SIDE LAKE
CITY

Cameron Esau

For Caralysa and Julia
And special thanks to my sister Jennifer

http://www.sidelakecity.ca/   facebook.com/Side-Lake-City

 FriesenPress

Suite 300 - 990 Fort St
Victoria, BC, V8V 3K2
Canada

www.friesenpress.com

ISBN
978-1-5255-7735-2 (Hardcover)
978-1-5255-7736-9 (Paperback)
978-1-5255-7737-6 (eBook)

1. BIOGRAPHY & AUTOBIOGRAPHY, PERSONAL MEMOIRS

Distributed to the trade by The Ingram Book Company

DEDICATION

In memory of my father, Oliver Leonard Esau

We remember your love:
A love that was given freely…a love that never diminished…
A love that we never doubted…a quiet, respectful and honest love…
a caring love…a strong love…a love communicated through hugs…
a love that has become a part of us…
and when we see it, and when we give it, and when we feel it, we
remember you.

From a poem by Robert John Esau

Oliver Leonard Esau

Isaac and Esau sign posted on Highway 43 at Crooked Creek

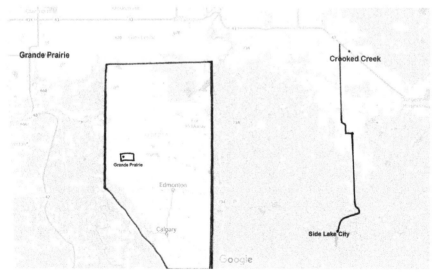

Map of Alberta showing location of Side Lake City

CONTENTS

FOREWORD

This is my memoir, the story of the adventures of a boy living in a sawmill camp in northern Alberta during the mid-century, 1950's and 1960's. It's also the story of my Dad's sawmill company, the land, the times, the flora and fauna, and the history of bush mills in the area including their eventual demise.

In preparation for writing this story I enrolled in an evening class on 'Writing your Memoirs' several years ago, we did a little writing each class. One evening we were asked to write a short story about a pivotal event in our life. It didn't need to be a major event, just something that moved us at the time. I was at a loss for something specific, and knowing I needed to keep it short and that I would have to read to the class right away I eventually decided to write about the birth of my youngest brother Robert, so I wrote the following:

"At the age of 10 I had two brothers, Gordon was 14 months younger and we were known as 'The boys'. After a sister was born along came another brother Donald, he was a pain in the ass to have around, not old enough to be included in our games yet he always insisted on being involved. Then after two more sisters came into the family another brother came along. Robert was the last of the family of seven kids, known thereafter as the baby! I was enthralled at the opportunity of observing this young boy grow up. I spent a lot of time with him, noticing him slowly evolving into a toddler and on into a small boy. I never grew tired of his company, I had lots of patience with his everyday antics. I took every opportunity to teach him things like tying his shoes and learning to catch a ball.

As I got older and into my teens I was getting restless to get away from the family and strike off on my own. Even the allure of Robert's presence was not enough to keep me at home and at age 17 I left with all my worldly possessions and moved to the lower mainland of BC. After six months the family was about to make a big move from the country to Edmonton and knowing I was needed I travelled back home. It was wonderful to be back with the family again, but I only stayed for two years and then moved away for good"

As I was writing I recognized that I had left a huge gap in the story that needed to be included, so I inserted the following sentence after the line about teaching Robert to catch a ball: 'A few years later two separate accidents claimed the lives of both Gordon and Donald, now Robert was my only brother.'

When it was my turn to read to the class what I had just written I did fine until I came to the sentence above, halfway through it I choked up and couldn't continue. There was complete silence in the room as I struggled to control my emotions which I finally did and then, embarrassed, I finished the story. I looked up at the teacher and said "I was not planning on going there". She replied that that was the thing about writing memoirs, you need to let the story tell itself and sometimes it does take you places you were not planning on.

It was suggested to me by my writing teacher that it was really two stories and as such should be separated, one story about the production of lumber under tough conditions, the other about a boy growing up in the resulting surroundings. I chose to tell the story all in one, as to me it is all one story intertwined with my early life.

When I started this process of writing about Isaac and Esau Lumber Company I went about gathering lots of facts of who worked for the mill and when they did so. I started my story with the principle players involved, the economic times, a broad description of the country involved, etc. Then I starting writing short stories about my memories of living at the mill, including of course Gordon and Donald wherever they fit in. I have concentrated mostly on the years at Side Lake, 1956 to 1962, but have included the start of the company in 1946 and continuing to its demise in 1966. I did not intend to make this a story of the loss of my brothers, I find that a very painful time to write about. Besides, they died in 1964, just about at the end of our sawmill story. I knew that at some point I would have to mention their passing, but just as an aside to the main story.

This story is starting to tell itself, so much so that I can no longer avoid the fact that my brother's deaths was the most significant event in my life. As such it will play a larger part of this story. As we age we get new perspectives on our past experiences, I think age liberates, I could not have written this story 40 years ago. I will now try to tell my story no matter where it takes me.

In researching this story I have relied heavily on the writings of my grandfather John Esau and two of my uncles, Edwin Esau and Henry Isaac, they all wrote extensively about their lives'. My Dad and Pete Isaac did not leave any written thoughts behind, nor my uncle Alvie whom I talked to a few years ago, but his memory was poor. Uncle Philip Isaac left some writings which have been a great help. Abe Isaac sadly passed away far too young to leave behind any written thoughts.

Assembling pictures from the earlier years of Isaac and Esau was a challenge, the church they belonged to forbade photography. Still, there were a lot of rebels like my dad who became an amateur photographer in the mid 50's.

COMPANY OF EIGHT MEN

Well I've been given a request,
And I shall surely try best,
Although my mind ain't no more keen.
We formed a comp'ny of eight men,
Sorta all from the same den.
Uncle John Esau with his sons,
And us four Isaac's all as one.
We bought us a brand new sawmill,
And parked it north east on a hill.
I don't know where we got the cash,
We had trouble buying hash,
But we got going, we did somehow,
With the sweat upon our brow.
The trees were owned by Hales H. Ross,
And his son Clifford was our boss.
"Twas him that told us what to do",
And I think we followed through.
The way that Clifford guided us,
Turned out to be a plus.
'Isaac and Esau' was our name,
With sawing spruce we won our fame.
Uncle John was president,
And me bush foreman as it went.

Pete and Alvie sawed the lumber,
Hoards and hoards, just without number.
Oliver signed the pay cheques sure,
As long as the comp'ny did endure.

Phil worked in the bush or mill,
He did it with a right good will.
When we bought us a Cletrac,
Edwin Esau had the knack.

He brought the logs in with great ease,
The whole thing seemed to be a breeze.
Abe took the planks right from the saw,
The sweat just pouring from his brow.
But one by one we drifted home,
'Neath the shelter of our dome.
I was the first to sell my share,
And I want you all to be aware,
I loved the wheel and shifting gears,
I hauled their lumber years and years.
Then Phil went home to his homestead,
He had a dairy in his head,
And he was a happy man,
Working his own ploughed up land.
Uncle John went farming too,
Edwin and Alvie followed through.

I wish I did not have to write,
About Abe; it was a fright.
When he was backing in the truck,
It just seemed it was his luck,
The load of lumber, it fell down,
And pinned my brother to the ground.
And our good neighbors all around,
A finer bunch could not be found.
They, all of them, sure did their best,
To put our troubled hearts at rest.
But Pete just kept on sawing wood,
And Oliver did the best he could.
He ran the outfit good and well,
And I don't know what else to tell.

My sister Mary was the cook,
And she was good in her own nook.
Of us eight men there are three left,

And I sometimes feel bereft.
I long for those who have passed on,
Into the "Great Blissful Beyond".
But time and tide wait for no man,
So let's all do the best we can.
Let's walk the Golden Rule in style,
We'll meet them on the Golden shore
Where parting hands are known no more.

By Henry Isaac
(Written after Oliver passed away in April 1993)
With permission of the Henry Isaac Family

Henry Isaac

ONE

LUNCH IN THE BUSH

Gordon and I pulled felt inserts over our socks, then moose hide moccasins over the felt and we knew our feet would be warm and dry even in the 20 below weather outside. Our younger brother Donald was also getting dressed for outside but us older boys hurried to get out ahead of him, hoping he would give up and stay home. Nobody noticed as I surreptitiously took a half dozen matches from the wall container and shoved them into my pocket. Mom and Maggie were pouring over the latest supply of 45's from town and just before we stepped out we heard the opening bars of Wilf Carters "Blue Canadian Rockies". I picked up an axe outside the door and then we joined four other boys, Gladwin, Delmer, Victor and Ralston, who also had an axe. Bright sunshine reflected off the new fallen snow, and a woodpecker drummed against a large dead tree at the edge of camp announcing its presence. The six of us headed out east into the forest, feeling very comfortable in our surroundings. We had only gone a short distance when we noticed that the younger boys Donald and Gladwin's brother Randy were trailing along behind us. Chagrined, I hollered out to them to go back to camp, but they ignored me.

The snow was over 2 feet deep and the trail-maker gave up his position every few minutes to get a rest, except for me. I lagged behind as usual, I was always a little on the heavy side and despite lots of outdoor activities I never felt as physically fit as the others and so I always struggled to keep up with the other boys. Most of us wore moccasins, and in the cold dry air our feet were warm. Parkas were pulled tight at the neck and toques were pulled down to keep the cold out. The bulges in our pockets indicated we had not come unprepared. After about half an hour, being far from the Sawmill camp, we stopped and looked around. A large crow cawed indignantly at our incursion into his territory, then flapped away in anger. I picked out a Poplar tree that was about eight inches in diameter and started chopping it with my axe. By this time Donald and Randy had caught up with us older boys and we grudgingly accepted their presence, although Victor told them they had better have brought their own food. I fell the tree carefully just above snow level and didn't chop it all the way through so that when it fell the butt end stayed attached to the stump. Ralston had also picked out a tree and fell it the same way, leaving a space in between about six feet across. A much smaller dead tree was felled and chopped up into lengths for firewood by Victor and Gladwin. The other two boys, Gordon and Delmer, used their feet to clear the snow out from the area between the felled trees. They broke off some of the lower dead branches of the trees, then went to a nearby spruce tree and pulled some dried moss off the branches. A match was struck onto a little bit of toilet paper and the moss and small twigs soon started to smoke heavily. As the fire grew it smoked less and more wood was added.

We boys joked around, pushing and shoving each other as we all got close to the warming fire, and the two younger ones pushed their way into the centre of the circle to demand their inclusion. As the fire got a lot bigger we backed up to the fallen trees and sat down. Several cans of beans, corn, and spam appeared from pockets and using our knives we crudely cut the tops off and punched holes through the cans just under the rim. After a stick was inserted through the can it was held over the fire to heat. The corn, with the juice still in the can, got hot first. The beans were a little trickier as they tended to burn in the bottom of the can. The spam was sliced off and either eaten cold or roasted over the fire like a hotdog. Gordon shared his can of beans with Donald. The food had come from the company commissary where each family had a page in the scribbler to mark down each item taken off the shelves. We all thoroughly enjoyed the lunch having worked up an appetite, and there was a lot of banter and teasing as we accused each other of being sweet on this or that girl back at camp. The younger two boys took a lot of ribbing about being left behind in the bush to fend for themselves! As the early winter evening started to dim the sky we trudged back to camp, making plans to meet after supper at the slab fire. As we parted on the street I called out "See you later alligator" and the quick reply came back "After a while crocodile".

Six of us boys were sons of the sawmill owners and the other two were sons of the head faller. The camp we were headed back to was like a small village set out in the forest an hour's drive south of Crooked Creek Alberta, and across the Simonette River. It was owned by Isaac and Esau Lumber Co. and called Side Lake City.

TWO

SIDE LAKE CITY

Side Lake City was a place where dreams were fulfilled and where ambition flourished. It was a place where men worked hard and women even harder keeping home and family secure. It was a place where boys played at manly things and girls envied them, then went and played at house making. It was a place where young men dreamed of girlfriends left back home, and where young ladies worked in kitchens delivering hot succulent meals to hungry workers. It was a place where boys came of age and girls blossomed. It was where I spent each winter from age nine to fifteen.

In the late 1950's it was a sawmill bush camp that was a noisy boisterous village all winter long then slept in silent solitude through the long hot summer months. It was a place where the air was bitterly cold at times but always filled with the sweet appley smell of fresh cut spruce. When it was fully occupied in the winter one noticed the constant hum of activity, the echoing shrill of the head saw as it bit deep into a log, lowered to a growl as the saw progressed through the cut, then climbed to a crescendo as another plank was released from the log. During the summer months the refuse pile was smelly and overblown with flies, while down at the mill the sawdust pile was hot and dusty with a mild smell of mould. The mosquitoes were ubiquitous.

The enterprise that lived at Side Lake City was called "Isaac and Esau Lumber Company Ltd" and it was originally owned by eight men, all related.

My Grandfather John Esau and three of his sons Edwin, Oliver (my dad) and Alvie were the Esau's. Four Isaac brothers Philip, Henry, Pete and Abe, cousins to my dad, were the other half of the company. The Isaac's and the Esau's were Mennonites, an independent, self-contained community with strong religious and sociological characteristics. The Mennonites had been renowned as settlers and farmers for centuries in Holland, Germany, and Prussia, it was the reason Catherine the Great invited them to settle in Russia in the 18th century. Her representatives offered the Mennonites economic opportunities and religious freedom and when my forefathers came to Russia in 1786 they settled near the Dnieper area of the Ukraine, in an area that already had a lot of Germanic speaking people. In 1870 the Russian government issued a proclamation stating the intention to end all special privileges granted to German colonists by 1880. Alarmed at the possibility of losing military exemption from army conscription, starting in 1874 tens of thousands of Mennonites immigrated to North America, a lot of them settling in Manitoba. From there they spread out across the prairies as the children from large families sought farms of their own. During war time the men were classified as Conscientious Objectors and had to do alternative service for the country, often working away from home in CO camps.

My Great-great Grandfather Johan Toews was born in Russia in 1829, widowed and remarried to Anna Warkentine (b 1831) in 1856. They had 10 children, the first four died as infants. Their second oldest surviving daughter Helena, born in Russia in 1863 was eleven years old when the family immigrated to Manitoba.

Another Great-Great Grandfather Heinrich Esau (b 1830) Married Anna Klassen in 1854 and they also immigrated to Manitoba in 1874, one of their sons was named Abram.

My Great Grandmother Helena married my Great Grandfather Abram Esau (b 1865) on April 5 1889 and they had 13 children, including two who died as infants. My Grandfather John was their fifth child, born on July 4 1895, he had four older sisters and four of each younger sisters and brothers.

John Esau

Although John was born in Oregon USA he grew up near Steinbach Manitoba. John was not a big man, he stood about 5' 7" but he was lean and tough from years of hard work. He appeared serious and stern at most times, but could easily laugh at a good joke. He worked at many different jobs from an early age, an uncle had a boarding house in Winnipeg and he spent one winter sweeping floors, making beds, washing dishes and cooking. He was advised to return to the farm after that to avoid military service as World War 1 was still on so he went back home. He took the train to Alberta and after working for a farmer for the summer he purchased a quarter section of land at an auction. John spent a lot of time living with his older sister Anna Isaac and her family until he built his own log cabin on his farm. During a Spanish Flu epidemic he volunteered to help the sick at a makeshift hospital where he met a nurse, Margaret de Veer, she fell sick too and John helped her until she got better. A couple of years later when John decided he needed a helpmeet (his word!) he looked up Margaret and paid her a visit. They were married on December 7 1919 and lived on the farm at Linden in southern Alberta where their four oldest sons were born, Edwin, Oliver, Wilton, and Alvie. Wilton died of black measles at less than two years old and within two days of Margaret's dad passing away so they had a heart-rending double funeral. Their first daughter Pauline was born at Bear Lake, near Grande Prairie, during their first foray into homesteading, then two years later back at Linden they had their fifth son Wilbert. At Crooked Creek they added to the family with the births of daughter Priscilla, twin sons Clarence and Benjamin (Benjamin died at birth), another son Harvey who lived little more than a year, and daughter Mildred who was the baby of the family.

The land in the Crooked Creek area was covered with willows and poplar trees interspersed with burnt out and wind fall areas, and some muskeg. It was raw land, most of it flat or gently rolling hills between creeks which ran down in deep ravines. The soil under the brush was rich and promising. The first homes were crude log cabins with sod roofs which leaked during heavy rains! The depression of the thirties had not yet been overcome and barter and trade was the order of the day, workers at sawmills often received lumber for their pay. They often brought home a moose or deer for the dinner table, the hunting laws were relaxed for settlers during this time.

By the time he homesteaded at Crooked Creek, John was good at farming, and an accomplished blacksmith and inventor. He hand built a Sawmill out of the iron from two Massey Harris binders, it had a Model T drive and also had a shingle cutting attachment. It was powered with an old Case tractor motor. He later sold it to Jim Airth of Debolt. He went in with neighbors to purchase a second-hand Cletrac bulldozer with a 50 horsepower gas engine, often operated by his son Edwin and used to clear land. He was looking for employment opportunities for his sons and nephews when the idea of a Sawmill was presented.

Anna Esau, older sister of John Esau, married Johann Isaac on April 2 1912 in Manitoba. They had ten children, Simon being the oldest. Philip and Henry were their second and third sons, Helen, Katherine, John, David, and Mary were next, then Peter. When Philip was only 11, Henry 9 and Peter 2, their father Johann died of an apparent heart attack when he was out in the bush cutting firewood. It was a devastating blow to the young family already living in harsh conditions, Anna was heartbroken and four months pregnant. Abe was born five months later, bringing the family total to seven boys and three girls. The older boys soon began working out for wages to help support the family, thus ingraining in them the lifelong habit of hard work. Their mother was a strict adamant authoritarian who used her older boys to help discipline the younger children. She brought her family to Crooked Creek to homestead in 1936. She always had a well-tended garden with lots of flowers and her grandchildren recall seeing her working in the garden bent sharply over at the waist with straight legs, weeding. One of her grandsons recalled how as a little boy he walked all the way to her house for a visit only to be chased off her porch with a broom and told to go home! Anna later married Abe Giesbrecht who brought two young girls with him to the Isaac clan, Helen and Margaret (Maggie).

Philip Isaac

Philip Isaac was born on Oct 8 1914 in his parent's home at Swalwell Alberta, the second child of Anna and Johann Isaac. He was 5' 11, very strong and a hard worker and he expected the same of his son's! He was an uncompromising disciplinarian and eager to make good financially. In 1936 he took a homestead in Crooked Creek, moving back and forth between there and Linden for a few years as he made improvements on his land. Harvest time often found him back in Linden working for Jacob L. Toews where he took special interest in their daughter Alda. They married on Oct 6 1940 and moved to his homestead the next spring. During World War II he spent 7 months in a CO Camp on Vancouver Island falling trees. He sustained an injury when a tree hit him and broke his collar bone. In 1946, he moved his young family of three to the Isaac and Esau sawmill in the Puskwaskau hills north of the community. They lived there for about one year, but he knew he couldn't both farm and work in the Sawmill so he chose to sell his share in the mill and go back to farming full time. He was the second of the eight partners to leave the Company. Philip and Alda had a family of eight, five sons and three daughters. Philip was very protective of the women in his family, woe to any of his sons who disrespected their mother or sisters!

THREE

BOYS LIFE AT CAMP

I have vivid memories of the exhilarating time I had as a young boy, living at the sawmill camp in the winter time, there was so much to explore and do. Of course my dad and his partners had set up the mill to make a good living for their families but they could hardly have picked a better setting for kids like me to play in! We explored the mill itself when it was shut down, crawling under the head saw and edger, getting our hair and clothing full of sawdust, playing on the lumber piles and balancing on the green chain. In really cold weather we warmed ourselves by the slab fire that burned late into the night, turning back to front every few seconds to get an all-around warming.

Slab Fire

One of my earliest memories is when Dale Isaac and I were out on the main street playing when we had to move off the road to make way for a logging truck coming barreling through camp on the way to the mill to drop its load of logs. Dale's dog took exception to the intrusion of the truck and ran alongside barking and biting at its wheels. It got too close and was caught up in the rear wheels, its lifeless body thrown off to the side by the passing logs skidding along behind the truck.

Sawdust from the head rig and various other saws was blown out a long large tin pipe, the end of which rose higher and higher, thirty or forty feet into the air with the accumulation of sawdust making a mountain of the stuff, an ideal playground for energetic kids. A sign was posted near the pile that simply read 'Mount Herb, elevation rising' in recognition of the current millwright Herb DeVeer. We did aerial summersaults off the top of the pile landing in the soft sawdust. Our clothing was coated in sawdust and when we went home and peeled off layer after layer we kept uncovering more sawdust, it got all the way into our socks and underpants much to mom's chagrin!

On the older parts of the sawdust pile, coated in a thick layer of snow, we tobogganed down the side, if a toboggan was not available we used cardboard boxes. The braver boys, including Gordon, tobogganed down the steep sides standing up much like current snowboarders, moccasin'd feet on a thin wooden board without the benefit of bindings going airborne over a jump at the bottom, the only control being the thin rope attached to the front of the toboggan! We dug out caves in the older parts, the top layer of sawdust was frozen hard in a thick crust and once we had a hole cut through it we dug out enough sawdust to make a space we could all fit into, it was always surprisingly warm inside the sawdust cave.

On Sundays when the mill was shut down we crawled under and over every corner, exploring the various parts and getting to know the intricacies of the mill. The slopping roof was particularly attractive as it lorded over everything else, so up we went. That is, up the other boys went leaving me behind as I struggled to pull myself up over the lip of the roof using a truss as a foothold. I finally made it only to discover the rest of them had already descended over the far side. I soon discovered that going down was a lot harder than climbing up as you had to approach the lip of the sloping roof ever mindful that there was no hand hold to hang onto and the truss was out of sight somewhere below. Laying down on my belly and slowly sliding down until my legs flailed in midair, my feet finally found the truss and I carefully made my way down, my relief at having reached the ground overshadowed by the memory of sheer terror on the way down!

I may have struggled with some activities but one thing I learned to do very well was hunt and snare squirrels. There was a small grove of spruce just west of camp that had been left alone by the loggers and that was where I set about making a little spending money. I preferred the solitude of the forest, I liked being out alone with only the company of the forest creatures around me. Eli Joyce, who had the trapping rights to this area and worked for dad in the mill, allowed me to trap squirrels and weasels around camp provided I sold them to him. Squirrels were very prolific in this area and I snared many of them, I would then skin them out and stretch the hide over a flat board to dry out. I mostly snared them using thin wire bent into a loop over a dead branch that I had leaned up against a tree to give them a shortcut up the tree. I would set as many as three snares on one branch and sometimes find as many as three squirrels hanging, waiting for me! I would set steel traps at the entrance of an underground den but they were not nearly as successful as snares. I was seldom successful in catching weasels but I will always remember the excitement of inadvertently catching one in a trap set for squirrels, I think it was intent on raiding a nest until my trap stopped him cold. The weasel fetched a full dollar from Eli, a lot more than the 50 cents for squirrels.

When I reached the age of twelve Grandfather give me a .22 caliber rifle, a Cooey repeater that had been Uncle Clarence's gun. It had a tubular magazine under the barrel that could hold about 15 short cartridges or a dozen longs, and I became a really good shot, partly because I could afford to buy lots of ammunition and practiced winter and summer. I had already been using an air rifle for years, but I loved the added range and power of the .22. I stalked the bush around camp always on the lookout for squirrels, I seldom got a good shot at one, but sometimes Ralston would accompany me. He had a .22 410 over under, a combination .22 rifle over a 410 shotgun barrel. When he detected a squirrel high up in a spruce he would wait for a good shot with the 410 that would usually scare the squirrel out into the open to be picked off with the .22. He was the only guy I knew who could out shoot me!

I also saw Spruce Hens (Grouse), they rely on camouflage and immobility to an amazing degree, letting me come to within a few feet before finally taking flight, a behavior that has earned it the moniker "fool hen". Once when I saw one on a branch about 15 feet away I decided not to get any closer, I slowly raised my gun and aimed at the body, then realized I would ruin far less meat by taking a head shot and at this distance how could I miss? To this day I'm still not sure if it was pure luck on its part but it ducked its head just as I shot, then lifted off and drifted away into the brush alongside a creek. They are excellent eating but no fools!

One day out hunting a few years later, just at dusk I saw a large Great Horned Owl some distance away high up in a tree, sitting and staring at me. I drew a bead on it, then asked myself why would I want to shoot that owl, but I had a rather callous disregard for wildlife at this point in my life. I had been frustrated at my lack of success that day, and told myself that in the pale light and the distance to the owl I couldn't hit it anyway, so I fired. This is when I realized how deadly a shot I had become, the owl drifted down to the ground on lifeless wings, I walked over and stood above it staring down in disbelief. I had no idea what to do with its carcass so I just left it laying there and walked away back to camp. I didn't go out hunting again for months and the memory of that shot haunted me for a long time.

FOUR

BUSH MILLS IN THE FORESTS

The timber that Isaac and Esau milled was part of the boreal region in Canada that covers almost 60% of the country's land area, and spans the landscape from the east to the border between the far northern Yukon and Alaska. The area is dominated by coniferous forests, particularly spruce, interspersed with vast wetlands, mostly bogs and muskegs. Over 90% of the forest land is provincial Crown land and these lands were available for timber leases, the Canadian forestry industry is among the largest in the world.

Wilderness Living Skills instructor Mors Kochanski refers to the area east of the Canadian Rockies as the Spruce Moose forest. The white spruce is a large coniferous evergreen tree which grows normally 50 to 100 feet tall, but can grow up to 130 feet tall with a trunk diameter of up to 3 and a half feet. The leaves are needle-like, ½ to ¾ inch long and very sharp- just try grabbing a spruce branch tightly with your bare hand! They generally grow on well-drained soils on the banks of rivers, lakes or streams, and occasionally in peat moss.

Moose are the largest member of the deer family and inhabit the boreal and mixed deciduous forests of North America. Their most common predators are wolves, bears, and humans, and unlike most other deer species moose are solitary animals and do not form herds. This would be why we almost always saw them by themselves. Their diet consists of both terrestrial and aquatic vegetation, they consume many types of plants including fresh shoots from trees such as willow and birch. They have a tough tongue, lips and gums, which aid in the eating of woody vegetation. A large population of moose can contribute to the production of a spruce forest when aspens, birches, and willows are eaten away by the hungry moose, and then young spruce will thrive without competition from the other species.

The area in which this story takes place is less than 100 miles north east of the Rocky Mountains, of which the spine is the border between British Columbia and Alberta. I always thought the mountains were much further away, you had to travel all day east, then south, then back west again to reach the mountains at Jasper. To the east of the mountains the land descends into rolling hills gently becoming lower and the rivers calmer. The Smoky River, a major tributary of the Peace River, flows north east out of the Canadian Rockies, in the northern area of Jasper National Park, and slows its pace as it nears the flat lands of the prairie in the Peace River country.

The Simonette River originates in the foothills of the Rockies, east of Grande Cache and flows in a north-east direction through the hills and the swampy forest land. Upon reaching the semi-open prairie, it meanders north-eastwards and flows into the Smoky River 6 miles south of where highway 43 crosses the Smoky. Its course is very tortured and twisty, many times it doubles back on itself and then leaves an ox bow lake when a spring flood causes it to overflow its shallow banks. You can canoe 15 miles to cover a distance of 5 miles as the crow flies! The Simonette played a large part in our lives growing up, we swam in it, picnicked along its shore making tea from its water and waded through its shallower parts. It has been described as a sleepy, murmuring and lovely stream with lots of flowers, wild geese, moose and deer along its banks. To our family it became a slithering serpent sliding silently along waiting for its next victim, little did we know at the time that one of its next fatalities would be a family member!

Many creeks flow into the Simonette including the Cornwall, then flowing into it are Harper Creek and Crooked Creek, the latter has given its name to the local post office and store located on Highway 43, 8 miles east of Debolt. To the south of Crooked Creek about 25 miles and just up from the Simonette River is Side Lake. To the north of Crooked Creek is the Puskwaskau River originating north of Sturgeon Heights in an area called the

Puskwaskau highlands and flows northwest into the Smoky River. It was in the highlands, in the spruce rich forest, that Isaac and Esau Lumber Co. Ltd. got its start.

In the 1920's, an American homesteader named John Bickell moved his family from Washington, USA to a farm in Debolt, where he started his first bush mill. The lumber was hauled to Grande Prairie and then shipped by rail to eastern Canada and the USA. With partners who also owned sawmills he built a planer mill in Grande Prairie in the late 40's, forming a company called 'Northern Planning Mills'. In 1953, Bickell joined with other partners to establish Northern Plywood's, Alberta's first plywood plant. Two years later, Canadian Forest Products, (later known as Canfor) bought a 50% share of the company. Later they also purchased Grande Prairie Lumber Co., formerly known as Hales H Ross & Sons.

There were many bush mills in the community that provided access to lumber and employment for many. "These sawmills gave settlers the opportunity to improve their immediate surroundings in the form of wagon boxes, hay racks, and furniture. Some were fortunate enough to build new homes with lumber, and many sod roofs were replaced with boards and shingles. Some homesteaders worked for wages but many of the early settlers traded wages for lumber. Some also provided their own supply of logs to the Sawmill in return for half the lumber, the other half was taken as payment for sawing the logs into lumber. School taxes owed were sometimes paid in lumber, and lumber was also donated to build a church, hall etc. It was during this time that the currency 'wooden money' became the known name for the practice of exchanging wages for lumber. Homestead permits allowed each homesteader 10,000 BFM per year. The first permit cost $1.00 and each subsequent permit cost $10.00" (paraphrased from page 478 of Bridges to the Past.)

Transporting the lumber to Grande Prairie became much more efficient when the new bridge over the Smoky River opened on August 17 1949. It was a day of celebration with over 12,000 people from the Peace River Country attending. There was a parade across the new bridge, then later a BBQ and dance. Prior to the new bridge travelers always waited, for the ferry when it ran, for floods to subside, for spring ice flows to disappear, for the ferryman to respond to their calls from the opposite shore. Well after freeze up in the fall when the ice was thick enough a road was cleared across the river, but there were times in spring and fall when all traffic came to a standstill. All that was quickly a distant memory as vehicles crossed over the river in seconds and continued on to Grande Prairie, shortening the trip to less than an hour from Crooked Creek.

The years after 1945 saw new resource-based development, rapid urbanization and dramatic increases in standards of living. Ottawa also reduced or removed many tariffs and so lumbering and pulp and paper expanded, and most of the time did well because of the North American post war construction booms.

FIVE

PLAYING ON ICE AND SNOW

Dad would pick up supplies for camp in Grande Prairie, usually on Saturday, and about once a month he would return to camp with a rented projector and a few films, usually documentaries from the National Film Board of Canada and a cartoon or two. The word would spread around camp like wildfire and we would don our best clothes and slick our hair back to look good, then all gather in the cookhouse dining hall for the evening's entertainment. Dad always made sure the film's contents were suitable for the religious mores of the families, and for us kids. We learned about Eskimos in northern Canada, about maple sugar in Quebec, adventures up rivers and fishing on the ocean. We saw how logging was done back east when logs were floated down fast flowing rivers, and how logging giant timber in BC and Oregon was done using spar trees. But most of all we looked forward to the cartoons, Mickey and Minnie Mouse, Huckleberry Hound and Yogi Bear, Bugs Bunny, and The Roadrunner continuously trouncing the coyote.

One film that was very memorable for me was because of the music, the background track was the song "Cool Water" and I had never heard it before, I loved it! I really don't remember what the film was about other than showing a fast running stream and the music, its lyrics are actually about a man and his mule Dan in the desert wishing for water!

One Sunday, Delmer and Gladwin had been so impressed with the film about the use of a spar tree for logging that they decided to make one! They chose the biggest spruce tree they could find close to camp, and de-limbed it about eighty percent up, with axes, and then Delmer went up with his trusty axe and topped the tree. They accomplished this feat without hard hats, steel toed boots, or any other safety equipment and survived unhurt!

At Christmas time we made the journey out to Crooked Creek several times for church services and to visit relatives. Christmas dinner was usually at home with friends and family and we always ate well! In our house Christmas presents were usually left on the dining table on our plates that we had set out the night before. This was before we started putting up a Christmas tree which didn't happen until much later, when I was in my mid-teens.

I'll never forget the Christmas that Gordon and I got a table top hockey game, the kind that you manipulated the players by twirling knobs on each end of the game. The puck was a marble and the goalie had a lever that moved it back and forth in front of the net. We were very excited and played with it a lot, hour after hour with Donald squeezing in every once in a while to get his turn. Then word got out around camp and we soon had company, some of the young men working for Dad come in to play and they quickly set up a tournament, competition was stiff and the excitement was palpable throughout the house. Gordon and I got shuffled aside and were relegated to just watching, but we didn't mind, it was fun to watch the young men get all excited about winning a game! Another year and another favorite present was a Meccano set, we loved it and spent many hours building tractors, cranes, trucks, etc.

New Year's celebrations were usually as noisy as possible, those that had large caliber rifles stocked up on ammunition, women and kids got out pots and pans, and I declared that I would ring the cookhouse bell long and hard. I was really excited, we got to stay up late and celebrate with the adults! The tension rose as it neared midnight, everyone was out in the street shivering with the cold but determined to ring in the New Year. I grasped the bell rope as the countdown started, I could hardly contain myself. As the guns went off and the pots rang out I pulled hard on the bell rope only to hear a muted clang then silence from the bell, I had never rung it before and didn't know it took a gentle pull to ring it, I thought the harder I pulled the louder it would be! I had pulled the bell right off its bracket, it would not ring again until it was fixed some weeks later! I went outside to join in the celebrations, pretending nothing untoward had happened to the bell, but the next day I suffered the jeers of my peers as I stood out in the street shivering as much with self-disgust as the cold.

It was already snowing on New Year's Eve and it kept on snowing for days after, the flakes drifting lazily down day after day, light and powdery. Snow covered the trees and houses in a soft white mantle and when you turned your face up the snow fell on it light and gentle as a secret kiss. Silence reigned at night as the snow muffled everything, absorbing all sound, then on cold morning's squeaking footsteps were heard as the first ones up went about their daily chores.

The average snowfall all winter was 5 feet, and sometimes it seemed as if it all came at once. Every morning the crew had to clear off the lumber piles and green chain, the only parts of the mill not covered, and the only place not covered in snow was the remains of the slab fire, still smoldering after burning all night. The Cats were set to work clearing snow off the bucking yard and Main Street, then dozed snow all along the logging road on their way out into the bush.

One day when Leroy and his choker man Paul were finished early pulling trees out of the bush close to the west side of the lake they got the idea to make trails on the ice by pushing the snow off with the Cat. The ice was frozen nice and deep so there was no danger of falling through, they soon had a smooth racetrack around one end of the lake. That evening those workers who had vehicles at camp were soon speeding around the track, sometimes towing a daredevil on a sled.

Sledding was a passion at camp, we built small personal bob sleds from one by four's and nailed strapping metal to the runners making them very fast. We used the logging road to sled down, as they were very nicely polished from the logging trucks skidding logs down them. We had to watch out for logging trucks coming around the corner, and we often went sailing off the road on sharp curves and into the forest. Somehow we all survived unhurt! Gladwin remembers when the young workers built a huge bobsled one day, and hooked it and several of the small sleds to the bumper of a pickup, the driver was young and inexperienced and took everyone around a curve too fast. A runner on the big bobsled broke and everybody went flying off into the trees! No serious injuries, so they all climbed into the back of the pickup and went laughing back to camp.

We spent more time playing outside than in, we dressed for the cold and didn't seem to mind it. Every fall Mom would have us each stand on a blank sheet of paper and draw a line around our bare foot, this drawing was then passed on to a native woman who would make a pair of moccasins to fit. We got a new pair each winter as they never lasted longer than that, I loved the smell of freshly tanned moose hide!

We made stilts out of scrap lumber, a 2" X 2" would serve as the upright, the top end would get carved round and smooth for the hands to hang onto, they were about 6 feet tall and a couple of feet up would be a sturdy piece of wood nailed on for a foothold, we could then walk around being taller even than adults!

The cleared ice on the lake became a big hit and Saturday nights would often be spent on the lake skating around late into the evening, the area lit up with automobile headlights. One memorable night the northern lights were putting on a dazzling display, the whole northern half of the sky was lit up in brilliant colors and the headlights were turned off. We all marveled at the incredible light show, mostly greens and blue's, and with a full moon in the southern half of the sky the whole lake was lit up. We skated until we were exhausted and then headed home, the adults with their cars had already left for camp earlier, so we walked back, the moonlight casting shadows along the road hemmed in by tall trees.

Heading west out of camp one day I cut off the main road and took a trail just to the north of the logging road but parallel to it. I was headed out to my trap line after school, breaking trail after yesterday's snowfall. At a point where the logging road veered slightly to the south there was a clump of poplar and willows that had been leaned over and left by the side of the road. As I passed by I noticed a cavity under the trees, I crawled in and cleared out a few branches from the centre of the space and used them to erect walls on the sides. With a handful of boughs from a nearby spruce layered on top and the sides, I soon had a small enclosed cave that I could sit up in, to enter it I had to stoop down to ground level and crawl in. Pleased with what I had created I couldn't wait to tell Gordon about it. I found him playing with the other boys in camp and led them all back to my den. We found that we could all fit into the hollow space and with a combined effort we soon had more boughs lining the floor and walls to make a snug bear den, then after the next day's snowfall covered it all over in a blanket and with the combined heat of 6 or 7 boys it got cozy and warm inside. It became a favourite meeting place and we spent many hours sitting around inside, girls were forbidden to enter! Donald and Randy were sometimes allowed in!

My grade nine teacher at Ridgevalley that year was an imported Australian (Mr. Cropley?) who had taught us to sing Waltzing Matilda. We found it a catching tune and often hummed a few bars, then when we heard a logging truck coming down the road and passing a few feet away we burst out in song,

Waltzing Matilda, Waltzing Matilda,

You'll come a-waltzing matilda with me.

And he sang as he watched and waited till his billy boiled

You'll come a waltzing matilda with me.

Every time after that when we heard a vehicle passing by we serenaded it at the top of our lungs with Waltzing Matilda!

SIX

THE START

After the war ended the young men in the local area had little to look forward to for employment, then someone suggested a Sawmill, an idea that quickly gained approval. They had to find timber to cut, buying the rights to logging was expensive and there were very few timber leases left available in the area. They decided to contract out their services and talked to Hales H. Ross & Sons Lumber Company of Grand Prairie (later called Grande Prairie Lumber Co.) who, although as Grandfather John said "they looked somewhat squint eyed at us, but kindly," gave them a chance sawing timber north of Crooked Creek in the Puskwaskau highlands. Hales H. Ross and Sons had a large timber berth and contracted several outfits like Ernie Bartell, brothers Edwin and Fred Enns, and others. In the summer of 1946 Isaac and Esau Lumber Co. Ltd was formed with John Esau as President and Henry Isaac as Bush Foreman.

Henry was born on June 12 1916, the third son of Anna and Johann Isaac. The family lived in the Linden area for a few years, then moved to Manitoba. After his father's death the family moved back to Alberta. By the time he was 11 he was staying with neighboring farmers to help out, but still went to school as well, till he completed grade 6. In 1936 He accompanied his brother Philip to Crooked Creek and filed on a Homestead. He moved back and forth between there and Linden working for various farmers until 1939 when he went back to Linden to get married to Margaret Toews, sister to Alda, on October 29. He and Margaret had a family of eleven, eight daughters and three sons. They moved to Crooked Creek in 1944 where he occasionally found work in a Sawmill doing jobs like falling, canting, and driving truck. He was in charge of getting logs to the mill when Isaac and Esau first started. He was the first to leave the company, selling his share to buy a truck. He then hauled lumber for the company for eleven years, also hauling lumber for other mills, namely Charlie Moon, Burrows, Nilsson Brothers, We Three Sawmill and others.

Henry Isaac

Henry was an average sized man standing about 5'10, but his nature was anything but average! He was very outgoing and sociable, very much the avuncular gentleman, he always had a story to tell. His quick smile and friendly demeanor appealed to everyone, I always enjoyed our visits. As well as farming he was a truck driver almost all his life, taking a spell for a few years when he drove school bus for students at Ridgevalley School.

My Grandfather relates "The problem of financing was a big item, as we had very little money. One day I went to the banker, put our plans before him and told him what we needed. Just imagine what he told me, 'You Mennonites may be alright for farming but you are no good in business.'

That was all the help I got and it was somewhat aggravating. I thought that if he would give us a chance maybe he could learn something too! Then we found a company in Edmonton that would sell us a mill with so much down and the balance in payments, so we scraped all the money together to make a down payment." And so it was that the first sawmill head rig and carriage was purchased new in Edmonton, a Belsaw brand mill that was capable of sawing logs up to 16 ft. long. They used an old Chrysler car motor and Grandfathers John Deere tractor to power the mill, and when that proved to be too slow they added a Cleveland motor as well and sawed about 8,000 board feet a day (BFM, see Appendix one)

At this time rough lumber was selling for about $34 per thousand BFM, after stumpage fees paid to the Dept. of Forestry of about $10 per thousand they were left with $190 for the day. This at a time when average wages were $5 a day, with a crew of approximately 20 men they didn't have much left over!

They started on a small patch of forest on the southern edge of the berth and worked year round, using horses to skid the logs out of the bush. Working in the summer was arduous as the moisture of the swampy forest and occasional rain made for muddy conditions. The hordes of mosquitoes were at times unbearable! Falling was done by hand with crosscut saws and axes, the logs were then cut into 16 foot lengths before being skidded out of the bush. After two or three summers of battling the mosquitos and mud they worked winters only, the logs were much easier to skid on frozen ground!

In the spring of 1948 Alvie Esau was the sawyer when a serious accident occurred! Spring thaw was underway and the logs and bark were soggy wet. Underneath the saw was a metal chute that helped blow the sawdust away from the blade. In the wet conditions the sawdust was clumping up in the chute and clogging it. Alvie crawled under the saw to try to clear away the sawdust, reaching his hand up a little too high and into the spinning blade! One thumb and two fingers were left hanging by some tissue and he needed to get to a doctor fast. He and his father John got a ride out to the Crooked Creek store where they managed to get a lift from a passing salesman heading to Grande Prairie. It had to have been over an hour to get there, crossing the Smoky by ferry. A doctor at the hospital sewed his fingers back on and he was able to keep on working although those fingers were always a little stiff.

Alvie Esau

Alvie was the third son of John and Margaret Esau, born Oct 4 1925 in Linden. He was four years old when the family homesteaded at Crooked Creek. He worked at neighbouring farms from an early age, once he came home from stooking and proudly presented his dad with the community's first ball point pen! When he was 16 he worked at a local sawmill skidding slabs away from the mill with horses. He married Rozella Schartner on Oct 19 1949. They were devastated when their first child Della died at two years old. Their oldest son Lyle was just 3 months old at that time, they went on to have four more children, two more sons and two daughters.

The accident in the mill finished his career as a sawyer, but he still stayed with the mill until 1954 doing other jobs, then went farming his two quarters full time. He was not content being a farmer, he loved to build and became a skilled carpenter.

Ross and Sons Lumber Co. sent trucks to haul the lumber to Grande Prairie, crossing the Smoky River by ferry. Income came in right away and they first paid wages owing to a few workmen. They didn't have to hire many men because there were eight of them who owned and worked at the mill, and they each only took enough money to live on, the remainder invested back into the mill.

At first they used the head rig itself to edge the boards, and had trim saws set up with independent power to trim the ends. When they added an edger to the mill production was much faster. Long logging would come later when they used cats out in the bush and trucks to skid the logs into the mill yard. For a time when they first started using cats they used a wheeled logging arch hitched behind the cat with the main cable running up and over the arch and down to a large bundle of logs. (See Appendix Two 'History of Caterpillar') Even in high gear the Cat moved little quicker than a fast walk, so as the distance from the felled trees to the mill increased, they had to find a faster method of skidding the logs. An arch built onto the back of a truck served the purpose admirably. (See Appendix Three, The Logging Truck)

In about 1952 or '53 disaster struck when part of the mill burnt down. The crew were all gathered for a meeting in the cook shack after supper when someone raised the alarm. They quickly discovered that the source of the flames seemed to be close to the edger which had just been worked on earlier. They managed to extinguish the flames before the whole mill went up in smoke although there was a lot of damage. They were able to repair the head rig and carriage but the edger was damaged beyond use, they had to buy a new one. After a few weeks of intense work they were back in business.

The mill moved further into the forest every couple of years to stay closer to the ready supply of timber, they had at least three different camps north of Crooked Creek. Most of the equipment was already mounted on large timbers that were easy to skid to a new location. The bunkhouses as well were built on timbers for ease of conveying to a new location. A couple of years after the move to Side Lake Oliver and Pete were persuaded to set up again north of Crooked Creek to finish off a stand of timber that Ross and Sons wanted logged. A second mill was purchased and Edwin Esau was put in charge of a newly hired crew to log and saw for a few months until they had cleaned up all the available timber. After that the new crew was brought to Side Lake and a second shift was added at night to try to increase production. After a month of trial Oliver and Pete realized it was just not feasible to carry on with two shifts, and most of the extra crew were let go.

Norton Bros. Lumber Company was formed by Earl and Clyde Norton in 1955, moving their operation 30 miles south of Crooked Creek near Side Lake in 1960 and operated there until 1966. Access to their mill was through our Side Lake City camp, us kids used to put stuff into the main street because we resenting their intrusion through our village. They owned their own timber berth, then sold out to Canfor in 1973. Alfred Reimer was their sawyer starting in 1960, he was described by Earl as being a perfectionist. They were very impressed with their crew, being 90% Mennonites. They were very hard working and dedicated and never missed a day nor made any complaints. Ralph Norton had a timber berth east of Side Lake, Clyde and Earl Norton's berth was southwest of the lake and they leased Isaac and Esau's mill for a couple of years. (Pg. 506 'Bridges to the Past')

SEVEN

ABE

Abe Isaac was born on July 24 1926 near Steinbach, Manitoba, five months after the death of his father. He lived with the family at Linden Alberta and was 10 years old when they moved to Crooked Creek. One of his best friends was his cousin Alvie Esau. On Dec. 7 1947 he married Anna DeVeer, younger sister of Peter's wife Florence. He was the youngest of the eight partners, being only twenty when the company was formed. Abe had started off working in the Sawmill as the tail sawyer, taking the sawn planks from the carriage and passing them on rollers to be trimmed. When he worked out in the bush as a cat skinner skidding logs he would watch for his wife Anna to show up with coffee, pulling their young kids Keith and Virginia on a sled. He and Anna were a very happy couple content with life as they raised their two young children. He followed in Henry's footsteps and drove the lumber truck hauling to Grande Prairie.

Tuesday November 14 1950 was Abe's brother Peter and his wife Florence's 2nd wedding anniversary and they were about to have the worst day of their life. Smoke from the metal chimneys of the camp's shacks going straight up in a thin line confirmed the coldness of the day, it was snowing lightly and the snow crunched underfoot. That morning Abe cheerfully brought in a load of split firewood for the stove and water for Anna to heat, it was a wash day. As he left the house and headed to work he was greeted by Albert Loewen with a hearty 'How are you' and he jauntily replied 'I couldn't be better'. They were the last words anyone heard from him.

When he had started hauling lumber he convinced Pete that using 12 x12 transfer beams under a load was overkill, that 10 x 10's were strong enough. He did notice though that the smaller beams were slightly bowed under the weight of a full load of lumber. His Cousin Clarence Esau was shoveling snow off the top of the pile next to his load as he backed the truck under the load. There didn't seem to be enough height for the truck trailer, then he noticed a piece of wood frozen to the ground under the load that would have to be removed. He crawled under with an axe to chip the wood out of the way and the axe glanced off the frozen wood and accidentally struck one of the beams. With a loud rending crack the beam broke, hit him on the side of the head and the tons of green wood came down on top of him. Clarence saw the load shift, then come down and his first thought was 'what a mess to clean up'. He realized then that Abe was underneath, just as Pete called out "Where's Abe?" They gave a loud cry for help and started to throw the lumber off the pile and were quickly joined by the rest of the crew. They were frantically flinging the wood away from on top of Abe but when they reached him he was not moving.

Abe was loaded into the back of a canopied pickup and rushed to the Grande Prairie hospital, almost two hour's drive away. The truck was followed by a convoy of vehicles, including my Mom and Dad with Anna and her two children. Pete rode beside Abe doing CPR the whole way. As they rushed him into the emergency ward his sister Mary, a nurse on duty that day, was told of Abe's arrival. The doctor said he was likely dead before the lumber came down on him as the side of his head was full of splinters from the shattered timber that hit first. Mary went home to Crooked Creek that night and slept at Philip and Alda's, joining the rest of the family in shock and disbelief. The mill was shut down for a few days as everyone tried to come to grips with the loss of the cheerful soft spoken young man. His two year old son Keith cried for a long time after, wanting his daddy.

In a conversation with Florence Isaac in July 2016 she told me that Peter never got over the trauma of losing his younger brother in such a tragic way, a sentiment that I recognized and shared. The suffering for Anna was not over yet, she was five month's pregnant with their third child at the time of Abe's death and when the little daughter was born in March the umbilical cord was wrapped around her neck and the Doctor was unable to save the girl, little Dianna died at birth.

Lumber piles on Transfer Beams

EIGHT

WINTERS WARMING

I woke with a start, something was changed and I wondered what had awakened me. My small transistor radio was humming softly, it had lost its signal again. I had fallen asleep listening to Foster Hewitt calling a hockey game between Toronto and Montreal, I turned and shut it off. It was a Sunday morning in mid-February and I should have been able to sleep longer, it had been decided last night that we would not bother with the hour long drive to attend church. Then I heard water dripping from the eaves outside, and there was no cold draft from the single pane window as there usually was. The air smelled different.

I lowered myself down from the top bunk quietly so as not to wake my brothers and quickly got dressed. Out in the kitchen Maggie was already up getting ready to cook breakfast. I excitedly pulled on my parka, not bothering to do it up. I started to pull on my moccasins then discarded them and dug out my rubber boots, the moccasins would just get wet. I stepped outside to be greeted with a blast of warm air, the icicles hanging from the overhang of the roof were melting, dripping water onto the porch. The snowbank beside the shoveled path had shrunk to half its usual size. For the last month the temperature had been well below 0, now the thermometer beside the front door read 40 Fahrenheit! It was a chinook!

I remembered from last winter a chinook raising the temperature a lot then after a few days it would get cold again. I rounded the side of the house and headed down towards the mill. As I passed the refuse pile a small flock of chickadee's lifted off with a husky tsik-a-dee-dee call, interrupted in their foraging. I splashed thru a few puddles in the yard and found Victor and Ralston were already at the mill playing on the lumber pile's, I joined them and we enjoyed frolicking in the warm air with the fresh fragrant scent of the spruce forest interspersed with the occasional tang of smoke from the smoldering slab fire.

We were soon joined by the other boys from the camp including Gordon and Donald and a game of tag broke out. After a while we started getting hungry and realized we hadn't had breakfast yet. My brothers and I hurried home and as we entered the house we were met with the wonderful smell of pancakes and cracklings. We were just in time, we hurriedly pulled off boots and coats, washed up and sat down. Dad said grace and 'amen' was barely out of his mouth before we piled up pancakes and cracklings and covered them with Rogers Golden syrup and dug in.

A few days later the weather was icy cold again and we grabbed our skates after school and headed down to Side Lake which had a creek flowing out of it. Beavers had built a dam near the mouth of the creek and raised the level of the lake by several feet, backing the water out into the trees surrounding the lake. The melted snow from the chinook had frozen over and the lake was one large skating rink! We skated out onto the lake and kept going a mile or more, there was a large group of us kids and the faster skaters were soon far ahead, I was one of the slow ones, lagging behind. After a while it got tiring just going on in a straight line and we started skating around in circles and playing tag.

It was exhilarating to be that far from shore and we reveled in the sheer joy of skating. As we headed back towards camp we veered off towards the creek and found to our delight that we could skate down the creek, occasionally having to jump over deadfalls that were frozen into the ice. On the steeper parts of the creek the ice had frozen into ripples making for challenging skating, then occasionally there would be a small frozen waterfall that we jumped down. A few times we broke through the thin ice and found to our amazement that there was a bit of snow under that and then more ice, much thicker.

After we discovered the frozen creek it became a regular haunt for us, it flooded often enough that the snow seldom got too deep for skating and we went for miles up and down, crawling under and over trees that had fallen across it. On Saturdays we'd bring cans of creamed corn, pork and beans, and sometimes wieners to cook over a fire we built on the ice.

Back at the lake some of the young sawmill employees would drive around on the ice with their pickup trucks at high rates of speed and do donuts. Us kids would hang onto the tailgates of these pickups and when the pickup went into a spin, we'd let go and get launched across the lake at about 20 mph! If you fell, no big deal, the ice was smooth.

NINE

VILLAGE IN THE FOREST

To reach Side Lake City in the wintertime you followed the snow covered gravel road that ran straight south from Crooked Creek, with a couple of jogs to the east, then made a few curves as it wound its way down the hill and across a small creek until it reached the flats along the Simonette River. It crossed the river on the winter bridge of planks laid over log beams that had to be re-built every fall as the spring floods would wash out the old gravel approaches.

Shortly after freeze up in the fall, when the dirt roads could hold the weight of heavy equipment, two of the D4's were loaded onto trucks and hauled south to the banks of the river. Oliver and Pete would have already taken several trips down to the crossing assessing the conditions, watching the ice slowly form on the river banks out into the water. The river would eventually freeze over completely but as it flowed all winter under the ice it was never thick enough to hold heavy loads.

Building the gravel approaches to the Simonette River Bridge

Spanning the gap with logs

Building the bridge deck

One of the cats was slowly driven through the water to the far shore where it started pushing up a mound of gravel from along the shore into a large pile, then it would start pushing the gravel out into the river to form a roadway. The second cat was doing the same on the near bank, squeezing the running water into a main channel in the centre of the river. A rope was tossed across the gap, tied onto the end of a winch cable from the cat, and the cable was dragged back to be attached to the end of a log. The log was then pulled across the gap and pushed into position by the cats.

They continued working until they had 5 or 6 logs all the same size spanning the river to make a one lane bridge. A double layer of planks was laid across the logs to form a roadbed. A short timber was tied up underneath to stabilize the bridge, and more planks were laid lengthwise to complete the road. They were usually able to pull the bridge apart every spring before the floods came, to save the logs and timbers for that fall.

On the west side the road continued along the flats and then curved its way up the bank, it was a little steeper here as it made a switchback on its way southwest up the hill and on into the forest of poplar trees and here and there a small stand of spruce. At the top of the river bank the road turned south again and continued on for a few more miles between high banks of snow that had been plowed off the narrow road. As it neared camp a hand lettered sign on a rough plank warned of slower speeds expected and then another sign at the top of a slight rise announced "Side Lake City".

Speed limit sign approaching Camp

Welcome to Side Lake City

The road came to a T intersection, straight ahead and down the hill was the sawmill yard while a right turn led onto Main street which ran straight west, slightly downhill with houses along both sides. The street was little more than a wide yard running down between the houses with cars and pickup trucks parked haphazardly alongside the houses. In front of some of the buildings were logs ½ cut up for firewood, lines of sawdust running out at right angles to mark where blocks had been chain sawed off. The street surface was hard packed snow and piles of the same to make cleared pathways to each house. The houses were all framed buildings made of rough sawn lumber turned grey with age and insulating sawdust, now covered with snow, banked up along the sides for insulation.

Main Street

The first building on the left was the largest in camp, the cookhouse/dining hall. Across the street were three or four bunkhouses for the crew members who were either single or were living in camp without their families. Set back from the cookhouse was a smaller building that housed the cooks, and in front of that was a hand pump for water set on a drilled well, ice forming up around the base from spilled water that had to be chipped away regularly. In later years, after a small building was erected over the well, plumber Carl Shartner from Crooked Creek installed an electric pump and a water heater with a shower in the corner.

The well was the main water source for the whole camp, but it was very high in mineral content and the taste was very noticeable, it took a while to get used to it. The hard water would not form soap suds and the inside of the water kettle would get a deposited layer of lime scale. Washing soda would be added to dishwater and for bathing to soften the water. Sometimes blocks of ice were brought from Side Lake to melt into water that was more suitable for cooking and drinking, or snow was melted for the same purpose. We had a large copper boiler set across two burners on the propane stove to melt the snow and ice, and a communal dipper hung on the wall next to it for drinking water straight from the boiler provided it had not gotten too hot!

To the right of the well was Pete Isaac's family house, then next was Oliver Esau's family home. A path led between the houses to the outhouse, then continued through a patch of poplar trees and down the hill alongside the machinery shops to where the D4 cats were housed at night. From here the log sorting yard was straight ahead and the Sawmill was over to the left. The lake was another half mile to the south along an old logging road.

Back at camp the street continued west and slightly downhill with a dozen more houses along both sides, with outhouses behind each dwelling. Behind the cook shack was a small building containing the diesel electrical generator that supplied power to the whole camp and mill. Electricity was used mainly for lighting, there were a few small electrical appliances but not too many. Only during the coldest of mid-winter weather was the generator allowed to run all night, it was usually shut down by Pete at 11 PM with just a 5 minute warning by briefly shutting off the main switch. Pete built a lean too garage onto the generator building to house his car, the heat from the diesel engine keeping the car from freezing up!

Dad in his office

At our house inside the main door and on the left side was Dad's small office, just enough room for his desk and chair, with files hung on the walls and a window looking out onto the main street. There was an old style adding machine on the desk, and a two way radio that connected us with Grande Prairie, high tech for those days! He also had a typewriter and in January he would get me set up at his desk with a list of all his employees of the past year and I would type their name, address, wages and tax contributions on to blank T4 slips in triplicate, I had to punch the keys hard to make the third copy readable!

On the wall to the right of the door was a row of nails partly driven in that served as coat hooks for the whole family, a long row of parkas and toques and below them a jumbled pile of boots and moccasins. Around the corner to the right was a short wall with a small counter holding a washbasin for hand washing. I loved to watch Dad relish in washing up in hot water after spending the day outside, exhaling air through his hands on his beard, water spraying all over! Above the basin was a mirror on the wall that we used to carefully groom our hair before going out to meet the world.

Moving ahead into the main open area of the house the living room furniture was on the far wall to the left, on the near wall just behind Dads office sat the washer and dryer. In between these on the floor was a large grate covering the below the floor propane heater that was the main source of heat, we didn't use a wood burning stove in our house. The large chrome dining table was over to the right side of the room. We brought all our furniture with us from our summer house in Crooked Creek on moving day, all the living room, dining, bedroom, washer and dryer, etc. All our winter clothes were packed into our dressers and brought along.

Maggie in our kitchen

Further around to the right from the wash basin was the kitchen with cupboards on the walls covered with curtains for doors, a window on the front wall and below that a kitchen sink that drained into a large 5 gallon slop pail under the counter. One of Gordon and my regular chores was to keep an eye on the level of water in the pail, let it get too full and it would be very heavy to carry out and dump behind the house, yet as teenagers we always put off what should have been done sooner!

A hallway from the centre of the main room led to the four bedrooms, Mom and Dad's was the first one on the left side, the boys room was next on the back left corner of the house, the girls bedroom was opposite Mom and Dad's, then on the right corner was the room occupied by whichever girl was working for us at the time. There was a small bathroom in between the two back bedrooms that had a metal toilet with a bucket under the seat that also had to be emptied by Gordon or I in a timely fashion, carried out through the front door quickly so as to not smell up the house too much!

TEN

THE TIMES

The mid 1950's was a time when wages were .75 cents to $1.30 an hour. It was a time when pin-up girls like Sophia Loren, Jayne Mansfield and Marilyn Monroe graced the walls of young men's bunkhouses, a time when U.S. President Dwight D. Eisenhower sent the first U.S. advisors to South Vietnam and when a young Jim Henson built the first version of Kermit the Frog. It was when The Detroit Red Wings won the Stanley Cup for the 7th time in franchise history, but would not win again until 1997, and when a riot erupts in Montreal when Maurice Richard of the Montreal Canadians is suspended for a vicious hit on a linesman. It was when Walt Disney's Lady and the Tramp premieres and Gunsmoke debuts on TV, although we didn't know that because TV didn't arrive in the Peace River country until the early sixties!

It was a time when Elvis Presley appeared on The Ed Sullivan Show and could only be shown from his midriff up because of his undulating hips! It was when Floyd Patterson won the world heavyweight boxing championship that was vacant after the retirement of Rocky Marciano, then in 1960 Cassius Clay (later named Muhammad Ali) won his first professional boxing match. I always lost bets to Elmer Cardinal when he supported the braggart Clay!

The Canadian Prime minister was Louis Saint Laurent and the Premier of Alberta was Ernest Manning, winning his sixth consecutive majority. The Premier of British Columbia was W.A.C. Bennett.

It was a time when the Soviet Union launched Sputnik 1, the first artificial satellite to orbit the earth, and Canada's Avro Arrow was unveiled to the public. At camp we knew little of worldly events, radios were scarce and were used mostly for listening to music or hockey broadcasts and only occasionally did a magazine make its appearance.

It was a time when old style Country music was in its heyday, Mom loved music and her and Maggie listened to all the current hits. Wilf Carter was an all-time favorite and got an excessive amount of play with hits like "Blue Canadian Rockies" and "You Are My Sunshine". Eddie Arnold with "Each Minute Seems a Million Years" and "Easy on the Eyes", Hank Williams with "Hey, Good Lookin'" and "I'm So Lonesome I Could Cry" and Johnny Cash's "I Walk the Line" were all heard many times over.

Maggie had a subscription to Columbia House and when the records came Mom and her would always get together as soon as they could and listen to the newest deliveries over and over, sometimes to the annoyance of others in the house! Other singers of the times were Patsy Kline (Walkin After Midnight, I Fall to Pieces and Crazy), Ferlin Husky (Wings of a Dove), The Carter Family (Wabash Cannonball and Can the Circle Be Unbroken), and Hank Snow (I'm Moving On) who we saw live in a Grande Prairie performance.

The 1950's was a time when it seemed to have been the best years for Isaac and Esau Lumber. Company. Every couple of years, after we moved back to our main house at Crooked Creek, Dad would come home from Grande Prairie with a brand new car! He was a Chrysler man, usually buying Plymouths, a new one in 1955 (a station wagon!), again in 1957 and then in 1960 a Plymouth Fury with a powerful V8! A bright silver colour with large tail fins, its automatic transmission was manipulated with push buttons mounted on the upper left end of the dashboard.

It was a time when I turned 10 (1957) and felt proud to have more responsibilities and expectations, to be allowed to openly carry matches and take my air rifle out hunting. I felt like I was growing up and I noticed in school in grade 5 we all seemed to be a little more mature. My sibling rivalry with Gordon peaked in these years, we often fought over trivial things and when it came to wrestling matches it seemed whoever got mad first would win! Although he was fourteen months younger than me he was just as tall and strong but I did have a little advantage in weight! We never held grudges and would soon be best of pals again after a fight. Gordon always seemed very sure of himself and he always got along very well with adults, I was often envious of his self-confidence.

Things were a lot different with my sister Jennifer! She was three years younger than me but a lot cannier! When I got into my early teens she would torment me relentlessly until I would lose my temper and strike out. She made sure Mom only heard me hit her, not the annoyance of her behavior beforehand and I would be in serious trouble again! My brother Donald inherited our Mothers sense of humor, he could be very funny and often kept us laughing at his antics. Marlene and Lenora were two lovely little girls whom everyone loved, if they ever got into trouble Mom and Dad would be hard pressed to disciple them, they were just too cute! Then in the summer of 1957 Robert was born, the baby of the family! What a delight!

And so the nineteen fifties was a time when the Oliver Esau family was a happy and loving one, lots of laughter and hijinks, blissfully unaware of the hard times coming.

Cam holding Robert, and Gordon

Oliver Esau family, Dad holding Robert with Mom beside, Jennifer in front with Cameron, Donald and Gordon, Lenora and Marlene in front row.

ELEVEN

SCHOOLING

There can be few things as disruptive to the formal education of students than to take them out of their regular school in the fall and then back again in the spring, with an alternative regimen during the winter. This is exactly what happened to us 'Mill Kids' every year! We had a variety of teaching methods used over the years. For the first three years of my education, while the Sawmill was located north of Crooked Creek, I spent the winters living with my Grandparents so that I could continue my schooling uninterrupted. We moved to Side Lake in the fall of 1956, I was then in grade four. I had not been happy with the former arrangements and let my parents know! I'm sure they also wanted to keep all us kids at home, they now had the three oldest attending school, myself, Gordon, and Jennifer.

The first alternative used was correspondence lessons provided by the Province of Alberta, the regular curriculum was divided into weekly lesson plans that could be done at home under adult supervision. Every two weeks we would receive a large brown envelope in the mail that would have the results of the last lessons corrected by our distant 'teacher' and new lessons for the next two weeks. We had a one room school in camp that we would all attend for regular school hours supervised by Josie Thiessen that first year.

We kids were the Isaac's, Esau's and Judd's and whoever else was living in camp that winter. It seemed that nobody would agree to look after us two years in a row, each year we had a new supervisor! The second winter, 1957 – 1958 we had Ruth Reimer (wife of the sawyer Alfred) supervise us. The third winter was very memorable as we were under the care of Roy Mitchell, son of faller Walter Mitchell. Roy was only a few years older than us older kids and an intellectual, definitely not a disciplinarian! Bedlam reigned in the classroom and we all had a great time, then we were talked to by our parents and told that if we didn't settle down to our studies they would have to find someone else! We didn't want to lose Roy, so with his kind patience we all eventually got our lessons done.

School Bus and Kids, back row Donald, Jennifer, Caroline Judd, Gladwin Isaac, and Mr. Fast. Front row Mildred Judd, Marlene, Verna Judd, Randy Isaac, Gordon and Cameron.

By the fall of 1959 the number of students had grown to about 20 and the decision was made to hire a qualified teacher, no more correspondence lessons. A larger one room building with a wood burning stove in the corner was set up as our school, Alice Bronson was our teacher, teaching grades one to seven. The following winter the number of students had dwindled again and as us older kids were now in grade eight our parents were convinced by the school authorities to keep us in classes at Ridgevalley. A van with benches installed along the sides and back (pre-seatbelt times!) was driven all the way to school every day by Harley Jantz, a grade 12 student. Harley would drive us to school, attend classes all day, and then drive us back to Side Lake City. It was much better for our education to remain in school year round, but the one hour trip each way was gruelling, made more so by the smell of vomit in the van from some of the road sick kids, in the cold winter air the windows had to be kept closed!

The last year at Side Lake my Grandfather John Esau used the van to transport us as far as Abe Fast's farm where we transferred to Mr. Fast's school bus for the remainder of the trip. Moose were plentiful that year and every day we would see one or two along the road, usually on the five mile stretch from camp to the Simonette River, one memorable day we counted twelve moose!

The next winter the Sawmill was located at the Latornell River south of Goodwin, a good hour and a half drive away. Mom and the younger kids lived at camp that first winter, there was a small school house set up and the kids did lessons by correspondence. Gordon, Jennifer and myself stayed at home in Crooked Creek with a lady caretaker so that we could attend regular school. Randy recalls that he and Donald were the senior kids in school that winter and ran roughshod over the younger kids!

TWELVE

MOM AND DAD

Oliver Esau, my Dad, was born in Linden Alberta on Nov. 13 1922. His older brother Edwin wrote an autobiography that serves well in getting an idea of Dad's early years on the homestead. He was 7 years old when they moved to Crooked Creek. The family lived off the land by shooting rabbits and grouse plus fishing in Sturgeon Lake, and by the second summer Grandma had a large garden producing lots of veggies. Dad was riding horses at an early age, and went to school on his Uncle Gerry de Veers farm in a log building that served as both school and church. Mr. de Veer was both teacher and minister.

Dad was a fairly heavy set man and stood about 5' 9. He went to a CO Camp in BC and planted seedlings, then to Whitecourt with Edwin. After the war he and Edwin went looking for work at the local sawmills and found they had no snow in the bush to help with skidding logs, so no work was available. They did get some firefighting work that summer. Like his cousins Philip and Henry, Oliver also fell in love with one of the lovely Toews girls, Pauline, younger sister of Margaret and Alda. They married in Linden Alberta on July 28 1946. I was born less than a year later on July 5 1947 and they enlarged the family with six more kids, Gordon, Jennifer, Donald, Marlene, Lenora, and Robert.

Dad

Mom

My Mother, Pauline Toews, was born at the family home in Linden Alberta on June 13 1923 and grew up on the farm, one of seven girls. They all helped out with farm work, learning to drive horses, cleaning house and barn, gardening, cutting hay, stooking and threshing grain. Mom loved riding out to bring in the cattle, and also to help her grandparents with housework on Saturdays. She did well in school, once winning a wrist watch for her high grades then going on to complete grade eight.

Mom loved to joke around and had a terrific sense of humour, she was not the prettiest of the sisters with her buck teeth but she made up for it with humour. Even when she was in a wheelchair year's later one of her favorite sayings was 'I love work, I can sit and watch it for hours!' When she married Dad and moved north they lived at the saw mill right away. It must have been some culture shock for her, having come from a successful farm in southern Alberta with electricity and running water, to then find herself out in the bush in a clapboard shack!

Mom started having symptoms of Multiple Sclerosis as early as the spring of 1952. After consulting doctors in Grande Prairie and Edmonton that summer and fall, Dad was pulled aside to get the result. He didn't tell Mom her diagnosis until the next summer and by then she was pregnant with Marlene. That spring they left the kids at home and sought treatment in Colorado over a three month period, and again later in Calgary to no avail. By 1960 she was using a wheelchair, when it first made its appearance in the home us kids played with it a lot. Before Robert started school he and Mom played a game where he would push her hard in the chair then jump on to the back to catch a ride to the far end of the living room. One day when they were on a ride the wheelchair flipped over backwards pinning Robert underneath it with Mom on top. They were helpless until the hired girl came in from hanging clothes outside and noticed their dilemma and came to the rescue! They laughed about it that evening, Mom was always very cheerful.

I have visual proof of Mom being responsible for bringing a group of ladies to laughter. In the winter of 1956 a local teacher with a small movie camera visited the mill and shot a couple of rolls of 8 mm film that he later gave to dad. The teacher was filming a group shot of Mom and 6 other ladies standing around on Main Street in a group trying to look like they were not posing for the film! Mom is in the back row and when you look closely at the film you can see her leaning forward and saying something then grinning broadly. The reaction from the group is immediate with all of them grinning and laughing, one of the younger ones putting a hand to her mouth in shock at whatever she heard! I love that bit of footage, I wish it was clearer and had a sound track!

Dad loved being out in the bush so he was the natural choice to become the bush foreman when his cousins left the company one by one. He became a very skilled cat skinner and loved to pass on this knowledge, as he did to me when I was young. His method of management was hands on, showing his employees how to do the work correctly by being the first to tackle a job. Dad was the bookkeeper for Isaac and Esau Lumber co., he did the payroll and signed cheques and paid all the bills.

Dad was also involved in community affairs like when he was appointed as one of nine directors of the East Smokey Rural Electrification Association in 1955 and served for a couple of years. Electricity came to Crooked Creek in 1956, I very well remember the joy of being able to simply switch a light on at will, rather than light a coal oil lamp as I had watched Dad do for years! Along with electricity came telephone's, in 1957 a new slate of officers was elected to the Crooked Creek Mutual Telephone Co. including Dad.

Dad was not a very religious man but one of the things he really liked at church was singing. I remember he used to go to choir practice and I can well imagine him contributing his bass voice to the group, although he could probably also have sung tenor if that was required. The Holdeman Mennonite church prohibited photography but Dad wanted to take pictures and did so, he became an amateur photographer sometime in the mid 50's. He may well have been criticized for this as he seemed to lose interest in continuing attending church, especially after Mom was in a wheelchair and it became more difficult for her to attend. For some years after this he would drive us kids to Sunday school but not attend church himself.

One of the regulations of church compliance was for the men to be fully bearded, as Dad always was in the earlier pictures. He started trimming his beard, shortening it a little at a time, then trimmed away the sideburns. One winter day he shaved his upper lip and only left a goatee, as the picture of him seated at his desk in his office shows. The next step, sometime later, was to shave completely, thus making the bold statement to one and all that he was no longer a member of the congregation!

Dad often visited his parents and us kids frequently went along. On one such visit I was excited to be going as there was guaranteed to be a good sized forked branch among the willows growing to the east of the farmyard. It didn't take long to find what I wanted, in fact I quickly found two of them and soon had them cut off the main trunk and trimmed down to size. I stuck one in my back pocket to give to Gordon later and worked at the other as I walked back to grandpa's shop, skinning all the bark off. I trimmed and rounding the handle, then I cut a notch near the top end of each of the two uprights.

In Grandpa's shop I looked around and then found an old tire tube, already partly cut up. I spread it out on the work bench and carefully cut a long thin strip of rubber with a widened part in the center of the 18 inch long band. I tied one end of the rubber band to each end of the uprights and just like that I had a slingshot! It was easy to find lots of small pebbles around the yard and I was soon practicing shooting stones at various objects around the yard, getting the feel of my new weapon. I enjoyed hearing the loud ping sound when I hit a tin can or even the propane tank!

When Dad was finished with his conversation with his parents he called out to me that it was time to go. I climbed into the back seat of the car with my younger siblings and as the car slowed at the end of the driveway I took one last shot out of the window at the telephone pole beside the road. There was an immediate shattering of glass, bits and shards all over the window sill and seat, and the car came to a sudden stop as Dad swung his head over the seat to look at me with disbelief! The window had been closed! I don't recall there was any punishment for my act but I was acutely aware of Dad's resigned frustration of my recklessness!

When I was about 10 years old Dad decided I needed to learn how to start and operate a Cat, just in case. The 'in case' was never explained and I didn't ask, I was just pleased at the idea but also nervous and apprehensive! I paid very close attention to each of the moves he explained to me, afraid I would miss a step if I ever attempted to do this by myself. I need not have worried, I was 15 by the time I actually operated a Cat.

The procedure was done from up on the left side tracks, the first step was to start the small gas starter engine by turning on the fuel and holding in the starter button until it fired up and ran. There was also a rope coiled around a pulley that would turn over the engine if the battery was dead. Once the gas engine was running smoothly and throttled up to speed it was time to engage the drive gear and pull back the clutch to turn over the diesel engine which belched black smoke and popped loudly as each of its cylinders fired up. It was frightening and intimidating but also hugely exciting to be up on the tracks right next to the engine as it roared to life. When the diesel was running smoothly the starter engine was switched off.

Once into the operator's seat he explained the operation of each of the levers, the two main ones rose up out of the floor between your knees and were used to drive the Cat. Push them both ahead and the Cat lurched forward, pull them back and you went backwards. When you pushed one lever foreword farther than the other one the cat would turn direction. Now the most fun, pull one lever back and push the other one forward and the Cat spun around in one spot!

That same summer Dad needed to move a Cat out into the bush north of Crooked Creek, it was already parked a mile or so north. He took me (and Donald) along to drive the car behind the Cat so that he would have a way back without walking for miles! He needed to show me how to drive the car, a standard shift on the steering column. Dad got me settled into the seat on a pillow and had me slightly rev the engine as I started to let the clutch out, the car stalled! Try it again, he said, but with a little more gas. The car bucked forward and I let off on the gas then before I could push the clutch back down it stalled again. And so it went, attempt after attempt along the dusty road until finally I got the hang of giving it just enough gas to keep the car going and slowly accelerating. He didn't show me how to shift into second as he knew that in first gear the car would still go faster than the Cat in high gear!

Dad turned the car around and drove back to where the Cat was parked, my instructions were to wait a few minutes until Dad was a ways up the road then catch up with the car and wait again. Donald was all excited and cheering me on at my new learned skill, and in a clear case of showing off I decided to let Dad get a long way ahead then catch up by using second gear.

I knew where second gear was from having watched Dad, and with Donald's cheering me on we were soon speeding up the logging road, around a corner and there was Dad up on the Cat right in front of us! It took a fast braking action to stop before we hit the Cat and a large cloud of dust kept going past us and on past the Cat, causing Dad to jump and then quickly turn around to look behind him. All he saw was his 10 year old son looking all innocent and slowly driving the car as instructed!

I remember when I had a moment of clarity about how much I appreciated having my Dad around. I recall when my brothers and I were at an event with lots of adults and kids around including strangers, I don't remember what the occasion was. I do remember that when Dad arrived on the scene I had a very distinct feeling of calm come over me, it puzzled me at the time as to why the intense feeling. It wasn't until later after I had some time to reflect on it that I realized that before Dad arrived I couldn't totally relax because as the older brother the wellbeing of me and my brothers rested on my shoulders. Nothing was said when he arrived, no greetings or anything as us boys were all playing and goofing around, but I just knew at that point that Dad was now responsible for us all and I could relax.

There came a time when Mom found it too difficult to climb the stairs to the second floor in our house in Crooked Creek. Dad decided to take the top floor off the house and add an extension of 4 bedrooms and an office on to the west side of the house. This necessitated the digging of a basement and we did it with one of the cats, Dad got it started then had me take over. Using the hydraulic powered dozer blade, I lowered the blade into the dirt as I moved the cat forward, soon it started to stall as the blade was digging too deep and I slowly raised the blade until the cat started moving ahead again, repeating the process with each pass. Soon the ground was a series of humps and as the cat moved ahead it bucked up and down on the uneven ground and the problem just got worse. I looked around and Dad was motioning me off the cat, he took over and after only one or two passes he had the ground level and even again and then allowed me back on. We repeated this process over and over, he had a lot of patience with me as I struggled to learn to operate the dozer.

The next summer Dad was asked to get a crew of men out into the forest north of Crooked Creek to finish putting out a forest fire, I was put on one of the Cat's to grade and maintain the roadway/fireguard around one end of the area. As I lorded it up on the Cat over other guy's my age, one of them got tired of my obnoxious behavior and turned his water hose on me. I responded by backing the Cat onto the hose cutting off the water flow, it was a stalemate until someone said Dad was coming up the road and we all quickly got back to serious work!

THIRTEEN

LOGGING

Edwin Esau

In the beginning falling was done by hand with saws and axes and logging was done with horses. Logs had to be bucked up into 16 to 20 ft. lengths for the horses to handle, and they would be skidded all the way to the mill. Logging with horses can be very efficiently done resulting in less damage to soil structure and trees due to more selective logging. Edwin Esau remembers that on the downhill stretch sawdust was spread on the ground to help hold back the logs from running ahead into the team. Some daring teamsters would go full speed down a hill to build up some momentum for the uphill climb! After a couple of years they bought a used Cletrack bulldozer to replace the horses and Uncle Edwin was the first 'cat skinner'.

Edwin Esau was born on Sept 4 1920 at Swalwell Alberta and being the oldest son he quickly learned how to help his father on the farm, learning skills he would use for the rest of his life. He had a habit of leaving the farm without permission to go socializing and had to be reprimanded "right on my backside"! He was 9 years old when his dad took a homestead at Crooked Creek, he learned to plow with horses soon after that. At 15 years old he started working at Bickels Sawmill packing shingles, and later at their logging camp he used a team of horses to drag logs about 6 miles to the mill.

During World War II he was sent to BC Forest Service camps on Vancouver Island as a Conscientious Objector. The main purpose was to be firefighters in case of Japanese incendiary bombs, but most of the work was falling snags, pulling stumps, and planting thousands of seedlings. Later he and Oliver were sent to a railway tie camp near Whitecourt. They were paid fifty cents a day and their church also paid fifty cents for $1.00 a day in cash, at a time when a lot of workers were paid in kind.

Edwin was a tall lean man, he stood over six feet and had a very quick grin whenever he met an acquaintance. He married Irene Isaac of Linden Alberta on Feb.10 1946, they had two sons and 7 daughters. He left the mill in 1948 to farm, mostly beef herds that he drove out to the Simonette river flats in the summer to graze. In 1956 He returned to work for Isaac and Esau running the second mill north of Cr. Cr., and then working at Side Lake for a couple of years

Tree Falling was the most hazardous job in the whole operation, and the chainsaw is the most dangerous tool in forestry. A Faller is working out in the forest on his own, far ahead of the rest of the crew, it's his job to select which trees to fall and then do it as safely as possible. He had to keep an eye out for obstacles on the ground as well as way up in the forest like dead snags and windblown branches hung up on trees. He had to be aware of the lean of a tree and any wind that would bind the chainsaw in the cut and cause a tree to sway in the wrong direction. He had to make sure he had a clear path for himself to get away from the falling tree, as well as a route for the falling tree so that it would not get hung up as it fell. Another dangerous situation occurs when heavy timber begins to fall or shift before a cut is complete.

The faller had to be aware of any snow load, rotting tree parts or any other obstacles. Once down the tree could roll on sloping or icy ground. The Chainsaw could "kickback" if the upper quarter of the bar nose comes in contact with an object, instantaneously "kicking" of the chainsaw back towards the operator. The chainsaw operator may be trapped or crushed, a situation that did happen to faller Walter Mitchell.

Walter was from Fort Vermillion and his son Roy was our school supervisor one winter. He either didn't see the dead snag leaning against a tree he was about to fall, or perhaps he thought he could get out of the way quickly. When the tree started to fall, he backed up to get clear but tripped on a hidden log and landed on his back in the deep snow. The leaning snag landed across his legs pinning him to the ground and breaking his right leg above the knee. He lay in the cold for three hours before his workmates found him, they only came looking after he didn't come out of the bush at the end of his shift. At camp he was brought into one of the houses to warm up and get his leg stabilized before the hour's long trip to the hospital in Grande Prairie.

The first gas powered chainsaw at Isaac and Esau was a McCulloch model 5-49, the first mass produced chainsaw. It was purchased in 1948 by Dave Isaac, younger brother of Henry and Philip, who worked at the mill from 1946 to 1948. He also limbed and once an axe ended up in his foot, laying him up for about 8 months, finally getting a new toe joint at the University of Alberta Hospital.

Con Judd

Con Judd, part native Canadian from Fort Vermillion, was the main faller for many years and did his job well. His sons Ralston and Victor were my playmates at Side Lake City, and his daughter Caroline was my 'girlfriend' at a time when I was too young and naive to really know what that meant!

Three D4 Cats with Lorne, Leroy and Wilbert Thiessen

In 1952 Isaac and Esau Lumber Company purchased two new Caterpillars for about $4,000 each. A couple of years later they bought an older used Cat. (See Appendix Two for a history of Caterpillar) Skidding logs with Cats brought its own challenges, the cat skinner had to keep an eye out for his choker man who worked very close to the cat, pulling the winch cable out to the logs and then hooking up the chokers around each log. The Cat skinner made narrow lanes thru the bush to pull the trees out to the landing yard. The Cat then pushed the logs into bundles and made sure the butt ends were all even, ready for the logging truck. Unlike horses or even Cat's the logging truck could haul much larger loads at a faster speed.

My Uncle Paul Reimer writes "Priscilla and I spent the winter of 1956 at Side Lake, just south of Crooked Creek. I spent the winter as choker man, hooking the trees that had been dropped and limbed, to a cat driven by Leroy

Thiessen. You have to be careful to get out of the way, since the end of these long trees could whip around pretty fast if they were pulled around a stump".

International Logging Truck

The Cats pulled the logs full length out to the landing yard where the trucks came to skid them out. The trucks backed up to a large bundle of logs, a cable was slung around the butt ends of the logs and winched off of the ground and if the load was too heavy the front end of the truck would rise up into the air. The driver would be in the cab by now and rather than drop off a log he may attempt to pull ahead and start dragging the logs, usually the forward motion would bring the front end down again and off he would go, steering being a challenge because of the light weight on the front wheels! The whole bundle was then dragged, sometimes many miles, to the bucking yard at the mill. (See Appendix Three for more on the Logging Truck)

FOURTEEN

BEAR DISTURBED

The far off buzz of a chainsaw could be heard as the faller worked ahead of the logging crew selecting and downing spruce trees. A squirrel chirped angrily at the intrusion into its territory as they moved into the spruce stand, then the sudden roar of the Cat's diesel engine split the air. Cat skinner Leroy Thiessen bumped the blade of his Cat up against a large dead standing tree, then backed up and turned to avoid the tree. He then positioned the Cat's winch over the butt end of a newly fallen log so that his choker man Willard Toews could hook the log to the Cat. Willard then climbed aboard the Cat as Leroy skidded the log out to the landing yard.

What they didn't realize was that there was a bear holed up for the winter in the hollow dead tree that the Cat had bumped into and the Cat's activity against the tree had pulled a slab of wood off and woke up the bear. The angry bear followed them out to the landing yard, Willard didn't see it until he had jumped off the Cat to unhook the log. Suddenly confronted with the hostile bear he quickly jumped back onto the Cat beside Leroy, but the bear was very aggressive and followed them up onto the Cat. They quickly climbed up onto the canopy to avoid the bear and then looked around for someone to help them.

They spotted and then called out to William Wohlgemuth who was limbing nearby with a double bitted axe. William came over to see what all the commotion was about, then decided his axe was not enough of a deterrent against the angry bear that turned on him. He ran for the logging truck driven by Willard's dad Claude who had just pulled into the yard. Claude, seeing the two men up on the Cat just out of reach of the bear, decided it was time for a bigger weapon and with William on board he set off for camp to get a gun. Leroy and Willard, seeing the departing truck and thinking they had been abandoned, peered over the edge of the canopy to see the bear run off onto the bush. There was silence again in the woods except for the far off buzz of the chainsaw. The bear was never seen again.

That evening in camp the bear story was the talk of the village, and us kids really wanted to see the hollow tree. On Sunday dad loaded us all into his car and we drove out to the landing yard, then walked into the bush to the tree. It was an old spruce about 6 feet across, and it had a large cavity inside that went down to ground level. As we climbed into it we saw it was lined with lots of hair and forest floor debris. Seven of us kids managed to squeeze into the den, being in an enclosed space just recently occupied by a bear was very exciting and exhilarating. It's not everyone can say they have been in a newly vacated bear den!

The four easily visible clockwise from left: Donald, Jennifer, Verna Judd, Marlene

From the left: Jennifer, Verna Judd, Donald, Marlene, Cameron, Eddie Schram, and Gordon.

FIFTEEN

THE MILL

Peter Isaac

Pete Isaac had learned to operate a Sawmill at an early age so he was the natural choice to be the millwright and foreman of the mill. Pete was born on Dec. 6 1924 near Steinbach, Manitoba, the ninth child of Johann and Anna Isaac. After the death of his father when Peter was 2 years old he remembers his older sisters Helen and Katherine looked after him, Mary and Abe. Their mother was going through great hardship and the family was very poor. Pete remembers going barefoot all summer and wearing only homemade moccasins in the wintertime. He and his siblings picked Saskatoon's every summer, school lunches were usually unsweetened berries and dry bread. He moved to Crooked Creek with his mother and family in 1936. He quit school after grade eight and worked at whatever he could find, buying a team of mules and a Fresno to work on the new highway being built east from Grande Prairie. During the winters he worked in various sawmills and became a skilled sawyer. He was average height and build, quick and competent although he was at times rather stern.

He married Florence de Veer on Nov 14 1948 and they had four sons, Gladwin, Randy, Cyril, and Winston, and two daughters Eunice and Myrna. He moved his family to the sawmill camp every winter until 1966 when the company ceased operations.

"The Thing"

Pete tried to make a living at various things but was not happy until he was back in the lumber business. In 1971 he borrowed a portable mill and began custom sawing for farmers, then in 1974 he and Gladwin rebuilt an old sawmill that the Hutterites found on their land. They put wheels under it and made it into a portable and used this mill until 1981 as 'Simonette Lumber'. They hauled logs home from north of Debolt, then in 1977 Canfor offered them blow down logs, they rented a skidder and logged 2 million BFM that winter. Pete started sawing logs for log homes, leaving only one side round and planed on the other three by a planer he altered. A dream mill that he built in 1981 burned to the ground after only 3 weeks! He then rented a small mill to finish sawing the logs he had on hand. He sold his logging equipment to pay for the burned mill, thus ending his sawing career.

At the Side Lake mill logs were pushed onto the rollway by a homemade forklift, it was built on the back end of an early 40's Dodge truck by Claude Toews, he made the upright lift from scratch. The steering wheel and column were removed and replaced with a hydraulic lever mounted behind where the passenger seat had been, the driver position and controls were moved to the passenger side facing the rear wheels, the back window had been removed and enlarged into a windshield! At a loss as to what to name this contraption when it was first made we called it 'The Thing' and the name stuck! A second forklift was made the next year, again from a Dodge truck but a lot newer one, probably about a 1956 model. This one had a longer wheelbase for heavier loads and the lift mechanism was manufactured by Coutts Machinery.

Three canters needed on larger logs

The logs were loaded on to the carriage by the canters as fast as the sawyer could process them. Canting was one of the physically toughest jobs in the mill as they had to roll the log onto the carriage and then turn it to the sawyer's satisfaction with their cant hooks. When the log came back after one or two slices through the head saw they had to flip it over 180 degrees or however the sawyer wanted it, all the while also sliding the carriage dogs above the log up first, then down into the log to hold it fast to the carriage. They had to be quick on their feet, ready to jump over the next log in line to roll it onto the carriage.

After school or on Saturday's Gordon and I and the other boy's would come down to the mill and watch the men at work, we were fascinated by the fast movement, the noise, the smell, the strength and skill involved. The only safe place for us to stand and watch was on the same floor as the sawyer but off to the side just In front of the door to the millwrights shop. From here the canters were over to our right, the sawyer straight ahead and the tail sawyer and edger-man over to the left. We always came in quietly and slowly so as not to be noticed but after a while someone would see us and we were usually asked to move along for our own safety.

Sawyer Alfred Reimer

The Sawyer was the man who set the pace for the whole mill crew, there was a lot of skill involved in mentally sizing up each log as it came onto the carriage. The logs ranged in size from 8 or 10 inches for the smaller ones to over 3 feet for the larger ones, could be bowed and were invariably tapered from the small end to the larger one. Our mill sawed logs anywhere from 12 to twenty feet in length, the ideal log was about 2 ½ feet in diameter and very straight, 16 to 18 feet long with little taper to its length. The sawyer would take a slab off each side, then by reading the enlarged scale at the back of the carriage he would decide how best to utilize the remainder of the log. He pulled a handle towards himself that was mounted beside the scale on the carriage, it pulled the log towards him in increments and he judged how far to pull the handle to make a one or two inch thick board by reading the scale.

In the late 50's as improvements were constantly made to the milling operations the output of board feet per day rose gradually to an average of about 55,000 BFM per day, but the 60,000 bench mark remained elusive. After giving it much consideration a decision was made by the Sawyer of the day Alfred Reimer to try to make a run at a record setting day. The crew had to be psyched up for it as everyone would have to pitch in and work harder than they ever had. For a week or two before the big day the best sized logs, those ideally suited to fast production, were set aside. There was an air of excitement on the appointed day, could they accomplish their goal? A few side bets were made by those men who indulged in such activity, although by now everyone was on side to make a record day of it.

Arnold Wiebe was the trimmer man in those days, he was responsible for trimming the rough ends off the newly sawn planks before they continued on up to the green chain. Arnold was often a difficult man to deal with, he was lacking in good social and communication skills, he had the habit of getting very close to your face when talking to him and in his excitement the spittle would fly landing on your face! In today's world he may well have been diagnosed as high functioning autistic, but to those working with him he was just a pain to be around! He was often fired but was described as fireproof because there he'd be the next day, back on the job as if nothing had happened. He did however have a remarkable talent for numbers, he knew instinctively what each plank contained in board feet and could add the numbers up in his head as the lumber went by his station. He relied on a peg board beside him to peg up the lumber count in thousands of board feet, thus he was able to tell Pete at the end of the day what the output was. His numbers were cross checked by others as the lumber was counted again by the truckload when shipped to Grande Prairie, Oliver and Pete were often astounded at the accuracy of Arnolds count.

On the chosen day even us kids in the schoolhouse recognised something was happening, we were excited for the crew. At noon Arnold wouldn't tell anyone how they were doing, he kept it to himself! They worked hard all afternoon and at the end of the day Arnold confirmed that yes indeed they had sawn just over 62,000 BFM! Everyone was very happy and jubilant as they trudged back to camp after work, all in high spirits for their accomplishment. The record didn't last long. A couple of weeks later Alfred took a day off for personal reasons and Pete took over as Sawyer for the day. Pete pushed the crew hard, never let up all day, and at the end of the day Arnold told him he had sawn 63,000 BFM! He set a new record without any fanfare or preliminary saving of the best logs! The boss wins again!

Tail Sawyer and Edgerman

At the far side of the head saw the tail-sawyer would take the sawn off slabs and move them over onto the slab belt that shot them at high speed out onto the burning slab pile. The good plank's he would move over towards the edger-man who positioned them according to their potential width into the edger, again a job that required some skill. On the other side of the edger the tail-edger man threw the sawn off edges into the same slab belt then flipped the good lumber onto the trimmer chain, positioned so that the far end was sawn off evenly. The lumber sloped up to the trimmer man who positioned the near end according to the length of good wood available, then threw the sawn off end into a chute that took it over to the slab belt. The lumber then moved along the green chain to be sorted by size, pulled off and piled up into truck loads.

After us boys had been chased off the sawyers floor we would go around and stand at the other end of the mill and watch the slab belt, it was amazing how fast the slabs could exit the belt at the top shooting them like arrows out onto the burn pile!

Loaded Lumber Trucks

Side Lake Sawmill Camp: The two large sheds in the middle foreground are the machine shops where all repairs were done and the rolling stock was stored at night. The family houses are just through the trees and line Main Street on both sides.

SIXTEEN

THE COOKSHACK

A well fed crew is a happy crew and at Isaac and Esau this was very well understood. There were usually a lot of capable young ladies from the farms available as cooks, although to start with it was the wives and daughters of the eight owners who did the cooking. Women like my Grandmother Margaret Esau and her daughter Aunt Pauline, and Pete's wife Florence Isaac and his sister Mary Isaac, and Florence's sister Beth DeVeer were some of the earliest cooks. Starting in about 1952 Mrs. Claude Toews, Mary, and their daughter Josie cooked for many years, right up until the move to Side Lake. Breakfast was always a large meal consisting of porridge nearly every day, also pancakes or toast, eggs, bacon etc. The meal at noon was always referred to as dinner and was also always a large meal, supper was the evening meal served shortly after the mill shut down for the day.

The cookhouse at Side Lake was the largest building in camp, it had the commissary at one end with shelves full of canned and dry goods available to anyone in camp. Payment was done on the honor system, a scribbler laying on a small table near the door had a page for each family in camp, they would write down what they took from the shelves and Dad would deduct the groceries cost from the wages.

The next room was the kitchen, the stoves were propane. A cupboard built into the far wall had a door on the outside wall as well as one on the inside, between the two doors were shelves for cooling pies or thawing food or whatever was needed, the temperature regulated by either closing or partially opening the outside door to let the freezing air in.

The largest room was the dining hall with wooden tables and benches and a wood stove in a corner for heat. The room could seat up to 20 or 30 workers, those that took their meals here were single men or those that had left their families at home to look after the farm. John and Mary Shartner were in charge the first year followed by Maggie for a few years, she had a variety of help including the bosses Pete and Oliver!

Albert Loewen started working for Isaac and Esau when the operation was still north of Crooked Creek and stayed with us for many years. He had the misfortune of having been shot in the head as a child by an older brother playing with a .22 rifle. He was left with one side of his body crippled and he walked with a very pronounced limp, almost like dragging his bad leg behind him. His left hand was permanently clenched tight and bent at the wrist, and one eye was crooked and you never knew for sure where he was looking. He was usually as joyful as a child but was quick to anger if provoked. His right arm and hand were very strong, no one could beat him at arm wrestling! He loved to play with us kids but we sometimes regretted letting him catch us with that strong arm, he seemed to forget how strong he was and could easily hurt us and often did, me anyway.

Albert was very sociable and would walk for miles to visit with friends all over the community. As he got older and his bad leg would get sore from too much walking he found that he could operate a tractor so he purchased an old 1940's John Deere. He could now go for miles even faster than walking and he became a familiar sight on the roads of the countryside put-putting along in the old tractor.

His left hand being clenched so tight was hard to keep clean and was really useless, so his doctor persuaded him to have it amputated and replaced with a prosthetic hand. This was back in the 1950's and all that was available at that time was a crude hook and 'thumb' that he never did get used to using and soon gave up on. He used to complain that his hand was cold, that freaked us kids out because his hand was absent! Albert liked to drink when it was available, and although Side Lake City was supposed to be 'dry' it really wasn't, one weekend he and another worker got all liquored up and shaved their heads completely bald, I remember I was absolutely shocked and frightened that adults could act so irresponsibly!

Albert's job, we referred to him as the Bull Cook although he did no cooking, was to keep the kitchen supplied with water and firewood. He split firewood with one hand, then hauled the wood into all the bunkhouses and the cook shack. He also pumped (by hand) water from the well and delivered it to all the same buildings.

One summer members of his family started giving him a hard time about the fact that he didn't make the same wage as other workers at the mill. In a drunken state he came around to our place and demanded that Dad come out and fight him, he was really angry. Dad wasn't even home at the time and none of us in the house were going to go outside and face him. That next winter he didn't show up, Dad may have known he was not coming but us kids were puzzled by his absence. Dad then asked Gordon and me if we wanted the job of Bull Cook, Gladwin was also being asked by Pete.

So the three of us divided up the chores as best we could, trading around as it suited us, and were paid fifty cents a day each for the work. We had to deliver water in pails to the bunkhouses before school started at 9, making sure the fire was burning well in the tin airtight heaters with a pail of water on top so the men had warm water to wash up with when they came in at dinner time. Right after dinner we would look in on the kitchen and top up their water, then after school would be the bulk of the day's work for us what with chopping and delivering a full day's worth of firewood to all the buildings, and more water as needed. I didn't get out on to my trap line nearly so often anymore as I was too busy at camp, but I didn't mind, I made more money being Bull Cook than by trapping squirrels!

SEVENTEEN

SIDE LAKE IN SUMMER

One day in mid-July Dad called out to us kids "Let's take a trip down to Side Lake" and Gordon, Jennifer, Donald and I all clambered aboard the '49 Willys jeep for the day trip. Mom had packed up supplies for a lunch and Dad had purchased groceries for Soren, the summer watchman. The Jeep's 4 wheel drive was used as Dad drove down the muddy slope towards the Simonette, crossing a small creek half way down the hill. At the river we stopped for lunch, us kids playing along the river gravel bar and going in for a swim while Dad made a small fire and boiled water for tea, he always said that the river water made the best tea! It was a hot sunny summer day and the river level was now low after the rain of a few days ago. After the tea and cheese and jam sandwiches we carried on the last 5 or 6 miles to camp. In the hot summer air Side Lake city was altogether different than in the winter, with the flies, mosquitoes, and the chatter of squirrels nearby. Soren had heard the jeep coming and was waiting in the doorway of the camp house he lived in for the summer.

Soren Selsvold was a Norwegian who came to Canada as a young man, worked as a farmhand for several years before coming to the Crooked Creek area. He served in the army during the war and was wounded in France. After being discharged in 1946 he came back to his homestead, working out at various sawmills for years, seven of those with Isaac and Esau. He was a loner, never married, and was a friendly neighbour to all. He greeted us with obvious joy, inviting us all into his quarters. Dad carried in the box of groceries and Soren immediately offered us a slice of store bought white bread with canned butter, a treat. There was no refrigeration, and cooking was done with propane, while kerosene lanterns or candles supplied light in the evening.

Soren filled Dad in on the latest news at camp, the troublesome bears and the recent lightning storm that had hit a nearby tree but did not spark a fire. Us kids explored camp and marveled at the eerie silence of the main street now overgrown with grasses and weeds, so much different than the snowy white of wintertime. We looked in on our winter house, silent and empty now except for the mouse scurrying for cover. Behind the house was the refuse pile smelly and overblown now with flies, not frozen completely as it was in wintertime. Down at the mill we played on the large sawdust pile, hot and dusty with a mild smell of mould, until dad called to us that it was time to go home.

A few weeks later Soren noticed something different down at the sawdust pile. He knew there was always a little heat generated down in the pile, after a rainstorm he could see steam rising as the sun evaporated the moisture. But now there had been no rain for a week and the 'steam' had an odd colour. It looked more like smoke and as he dug down into the pile his fears were confirmed as he saw the charred blackened smouldering sawdust coming up in his shovel.

Spontaneous combustion occurs when a material like sawdust, with a relatively low ignition temperature begins to release heat which is unable to escape and the temperature of the sawdust rises above its ignition point. Open flame begins when sufficient oxygen is present, as could of happened when Soren uncovered the upper layers of sawdust. It could not be helped, the only way to combat this type of fire is to uncover it. He ran to the office and used the two way radio to contact Grande Prairie and reported the fire. The alarm was passed on to Oliver and Pete and they loaded up a cat and set out for the mill. There was no open flame, just a lot of smoke coming from the pile. The cat was used to level the sawdust and a firefighting water pump was set up down by the creek with the hose coming up onto the sawdust pile and it was dampened down. They all prayed for rain soon and it came a couple of days later, just in time to avert a forest fire.

EIGHTEEN

DONALD AND GORDON

Donald

Wednesday June 10 1964 was a warm sunny early summer day, when we got home from school Mom told us to get ready to go to the Simonette for a swim and a picnic supper. Uncle Harvey and Aunt Mildred Cardinal came along as well. At the river Mom and Aunt Mildred were getting the food spread out on a blanket as us kids peeled off our outer clothes, swimming trunks on underneath, and headed over the sand bar to the water's edge.

Donald was first into the water, Gordon and I close behind but as soon as Donald got in over his waist the bottom dropped off and he was in trouble. We shouted for help then held back as Dad rushed in to try to help Donald, and Harvey grabbed a long pole to shove out into the water. The current was soon taking them both downstream as Dad reached Donald who put his hand on Dads back to try to hang on. The current was so strong that Dad, fearing for his own life, shook off Donald's hand, then swam and grabbed for the pole that Harvey had pushed out into the river. Dad barely made it back to shore as Donald's bobbing head sank and disappeared downstream.

Gordon and I silently stood in the shallow water for a long time after, staring downstream at the churning water, praying that Donald's head would miraculously reappear. After some time people started to appear on hand and searches were made along the banks on both sides. Our Uncle Henry took Gordon and me under his wing and we spent the next three days with him as the searching along the river continued. The decision was made to send a boat downstream a lot further and that's when the search came to an end.

The Simonette finally released Donald miles downstream where his body was found washed up on a gravel bar. He was brought back to our home in the back of Cousin Allan Isaac's pickup truck, covered over with a tarp. I walked out into the yard and stood for a long time beside the truck, wrestling with my mind over a decision. I could see the top of the tarp and knew he was underneath it, would I lift the tarp and take a final look, or not. Part of me wanted badly to look one last time at Donald, to say goodbye.

I had overheard the comments made by Allan and others who had found the body saying how it was all bloated and white and hardly looked like the boy we had lost. After some time I turned and walked away, out into a spruce grove to the north of the house that was my quiet place. I instinctively knew that if I had of looked, that would be my lasting image of Donald and I didn't want it to be that image. I wanted to remember the laughing joking boy that I remembered from just 3 days ago, an eon ago!

A few days later we had his funeral in the Mennonite church, most of his classmates attended as school was suspended for the afternoon, and the church was just a short walk from school.

Gordon

Monday Sept 28 1964 I was making french fries for supper when I discovered we were out of ketchup, no problem I said, I'll go down to Froese's store and get some. I jumped into Dads '60 Plymouth Fury and headed out the driveway, I had failed twice already to get my driver's licence but that didn't prevent me from using Dad's car when I wanted to. Around the corner on the road I saw Gordon and his friend Terry Doerksen walking towards our place, I pulled over and they quickly slid into the front seat, Terry first. Once I had turned south onto the main road he put his foot over mine on the accelerator and pushed down, the big V8 responded quickly, picking up speed. I didn't object or try to stop him, I loved the feel of the power of the car and we were soon flying down the road.

Just past Chapman's corner I swerved the car over to the left side of the road to avoid a soft spot, we were soon speeding along on the left shoulder of the road. In an attempt to get back onto the main part of the road I kept steering further right until the front left wheel dug into the soft shoulder and the road surface rose up to meet me. A rough ride over the next couple of seconds as I went end over end, splintered glass and tearing metal, ground in front of me, then sky, and then soft ground and grass and at last it was over and I was still sitting behind the steering wheel hanging on tight, but the car was on its left side in the right hand ditch.

There was no one beside me, a quick check of the back seat told me I was alone. I stepped out of the empty windshield frame and scrambled up onto the road, saw no one until I looked south and saw two bodies on the road, the nearer one was Terry and I stumbled on to find Gordon lying partly in the ditch twisted and still. I sat down beside him, there was a keening crying sound coming from somewhere nearby, I soon realized it was me.

After a short time I was joined by passersby, an elderly gentleman suggested we needed to move Gordon up onto the road. Someone else objected saying we should just wait for the ambulance attendants, the gentleman said "but we moved them during the war" I replied "this isn't war". The silence that followed may have been uncomfortable, but I didn't notice, I was in a state of shock and time seemed to be standing still. An ambulance arrived and Gordon and Terry were loaded into it, Dad and I rode in the back of Pete's car following the ambulance into Grande Prairie. At the Hospital we all waited, including Terry's parents, for a short while then a Doctor came into the room and spoke briefly with Dad. His face crumpled and his eyes went wet, he spoke briefly with Terry's mom and then we walked slowly back out to the parking lot for the quiet ride back to Crooked Creek, Dad and I holding each other tight in the back seat. A lot of relatives were at the house but I ignored them all and rushed straight to my room, I heard my Mom scream. Some of my cousins were in there playing and asked how Gordon was, I replied "He's dead" and the room emptied. Dad came in and suggested that I go see Mom as she wanted to hug me.

For the second time in just over three months we had a funeral at the Mennonite church, and after a short time I went back to school. I often went out to the spruce grove north of the house, I would stand there for what seemed hours, just standing in the light rain or later in the snow. We had a small fire pit and I would think about lighting a fire. In my mind I went through all the motions of gathering twigs and moss, scratching a match etc. But I never did, I just stood there hunched over and feeling miserable.

Dad told me that the insurance agent in Grande Prairie was waiting for me to pass my driver's test so that they could put my licence number on the insurance claim. He took me in to town the next week for another test and this time I passed. Dad then told me that the police had laid a charge of careless driving against me, he went into court for me on the appointed day and told me later that the Judge had sympathised with his story, then berated the police for even laying the charge. The judge threw the charge out.

Terry survived, he spent a couple of months in hospital recovering and I only saw him once or twice after that, we never spoke about what happened. At school I walked the halls like a robot, no one talked to me neither fellow students nor any adults. I had a wall built up around myself. Dad tried on a couple of occasions but I made it clear I was not interested. He suggested that I should let it be known to others that Terry had put his foot over mine and pushed down, that perhaps then others would not blame me for the crash. I said "what blame, it was an accident".

We learned later that the cause of death for Gordon was swelling of the brain, from a hard hit to the head. With an almost hour long drive to the hospital in Grande Prairie too much time had elapsed with him in a coma the whole time, with today's medical advances he might have been saved but who's to know for sure. I don't think Dad ever really recovered from the loss of two of his sons at such an early age, he somehow seemed adrift in the world after that. It did not help when he was told by a church elder, after Gordon's death, that the reason he lost both boy's was because of the lifestyle he chose to live. That comment just solidified Dad's resolve to have nothing more to do with organized religion.

By this time the Sawmill was in its third year at the Latornell River south of Goodwin and the family stayed at our home in Crooked Creek all year. Dad lived at the mill during the week and came home for Sunday's. On Sunday evening I would take the car on an hour long trip to go pick up our housekeeper who lived out east at Sturgeon Heights, and along with a couple of mill workers who lived in the same area I would bring them back to our place. Dad would then take the workers along on the 1 and a half to 2 hour drive to the sawmill camp. This arrangement gave dad a little more time to spend with Mom and the younger kids. That next spring the Sawmill moved again, to Finley Forks in northern BC and Dad took me out of school to go with him.

Dad in his Office/Store at Latornell

NINETEEN

FINLAY FORKS

Pete Isaac with first equipment for Finlay Forks mill

Finlay Forks camp and mill

Starting in the mid 50's events were taking place in BC that would ultimately lead to the acrimonious end of Isaac and Esau Lumber Co. The building of the W. A. C. Bennett Dam on the Peace River resulted in a lake that would be called Williston Lake, it includes three arms, the Peace Reach (formerly the Peace Canyon), and the Parsnip and Finlay Reaches backing into the Rocky Mountains. It became the largest lake in British Columbia and the seventh largest reservoir in the world. As the planning for the dam moved forward in the late 50's the question arose as to what to do with the billions of board feet of timber still growing on land that would be flooded. Contractors were hired to mow down all the trees and haul them to a central location.

In the late 1940's Robert "Bob" Cattermole formed a small logging company in the Chilliwack Valley called Cattermole Timber, then in the 1950's began to expand the company holdings throughout the Province of British Columbia. He acquired the rights to the logs felled in the Parsnip and

Finlay River valleys near their confluence, called Finlay Forks. It was here that Oliver and Pete contracted with Cattermole to set up their mill at one end of a pile of full length logs that stretched for over a mile along the river bank.

We arrived in the early spring of 1965 and starting sawing timbers to use to build our Sawmill, using a rented portable mill. We worked long hours every day for ten days, then would take a four day break to drive back to Crooked Creek, a full day's drive each way. We kept this schedule for two or three months, we slowly built the mill with all the equipment hauled in from our last camp and then started on houses for each family. By summer we moved the families into camp and the long trips back to Crooked Creek ended, except for one weekend when Gladwin borrowed his dad's pickup, I took dad's car and with Jennifer along we went back to Crooked Creek for a visit.

Isaac and Esau Lumber Co. at Finlay Forks was a lot smaller version of previous years, the cats and logging trucks were no longer needed and sold off. I had a variety of jobs that summer and winter, tail edger man, piling lumber, trimming ends, running a front end loader, and every evening after dinner I would go out into the yard and do a count of the day's production in board feet, sometimes getting close to 20,000 BFM. Our production of lumber never got near what we used to do at Side Lake and then got even worse when Canfor made a deal with Cattermole to buy all the peeler logs. Dad and Pete were very upset at the fact they now had to grade all the logs before they went in the mill and set aside all the best wood for the plywood plant in Prince George, leaving only the small tops and crooked logs to put through the mill.

At Finley Forks I bunked in a small cabin with my future brother in law Elmer Cardinal, we listened to a local Prince George radio station every night. I really enjoyed songs like Claude King's 1962 hit "Wolverton Mountain", Pretty Women by Roy Orbison and House of the Rising sun by The Animals. We also listened to The Beatles, Diana Ross and the Supremes.

One winter evening I was bored hanging around camp and borrowed Dad's car to go socializing at a nearby saw mill. I parked the car in front of a large D9 Cat and went into one of the bunkhouses to play cards with the guys. A while later someone came hurrying into the bunkhouse and asked if anyone in here was driving a brown Ford car, I replied yes its mine.

He suggested I come out to take a look. I found the car had been pushed back several feet and the windshield was busted out, the D9 was nowhere to be seen.

I was told that a truck had gotten stuck away from camp and the Cat had been dispatched to go to the rescue. The cat skinner had not seen the car over the massive bulldozer blade and had raised the blade and proceeded straight ahead. The blade had cleared the hood of the car but broke out the windshield! I drove back to our camp shivering in the cold car to break the bad news to Dad. There was a 6 inch strip of window along the top that was not broken and Dad drove the car all the way to Prince George for repairs with just a piece of cardboard taped to the lower part to keep the cold and wind out!

Someone coming in to camp one Sunday morning reported having seen a bull moose cross the road just a few miles out of camp. An older worker (let's just call him Hunter for this story) and myself decided to go after it so we quickly packed a lunch and set out. I only packed my .22 as Hunter had a large rifle and a moose tag, I was only along for companionship and to help pack out the meat should we be lucky. Hunter had a lot more experience than I did and I was excited to accompany him on this hunt.

We quickly found the tracks were the moose had crossed the road, we parked Hunter's truck and started following the trail. There was less than a foot of snow on the ground and the temperature was just below freezing, an ideal day for a walk in the woods. The forest had been logged some years earlier so what remained were deciduous trees and lots of willows, the ground was gently sloping towards the Parsnip River with lots of undulations. The moose trail was very easy to follow as he was in no rush, just meandering along grazing on willow shoots as he went.

After about an hour of travel at a pace I was sure was a lot faster than the moose I was getting excited, whereas Hunter seemed to keep his eyes down on the tracks we followed I was looking past him into the semi clear bush looking for any movement ahead. We had just topped a rise and somewhat out of breath we stopped for a short rest and Hunter decided it was time for lunch.

I was quietly munching on my sandwich, Hunter had brought a can of beans and was scooping them out with his knife. The remaining beans in his can didn't want to come out and he rapped the can sharply up against a tree to dislodge its contents, the metallic sound ringing off into the bush! I was aghast and starred at him in disbelief but he seemed to be totally unaware of anything other than finishing his lunch.

We set out again a minute later and had only gone a short distance downhill and around a clump of willows when the moose tracks told a completely different story to previously. The meandering tracks came to a stop to be replaced with long strides in the snow. We had been within shooting distance separated only by the clump of willows when the moose heard us and set off at a run! We gave up at that point and returned disappointed to the truck. I was not in the habit of criticizing an older person especially one I had previously looked up to, but Hunters abilities, in my eyes, rapidly shrank.

Dad did not pay me wages for the time I worked for the mill, I was doing it to help out the family. He did give me a couple of hundred dollars at Christmas. By February of 1966 I was getting very restless and decided to move to Abbotsford where Uncle Henry and his family lived. I worked as a carpenters helper and driving truck. That spring Dad had also had enough of sawmilling and had moved the family back to Crooked Creek. In July I went back home to help the family move to St. Albert just north of Edmonton Alberta.

TWENTY

DEMISE OF THE BUSH MILL

In an earlier chapter I mentioned the Bickell family as being in the forefront of the forest industry in our area. Roy Bickell (Oct. 2, 1930 – Mar. 21 2015) was the son of John Bickell of Debolt, owner of one of the first bush mills in the area. Roy worked for his dad in the sawmill north of Debolt and in the planning mill in Grande Prairie, then for Canfor when they took over much of the forest industry mills in town. He worked for Canfor for 37 years ending his career as President and Chief Operating Officer, in Vancouver, in 1991, then retired and moved back to Grande Prairie.

I was able to have a conversation with Roy at his home in Grande Prairie on Sept. 2, 2014. I and some members of my family had always held a grudge against Canfor for the loss of our family's business, and I wanted to find a scapegoat to take it out on, perhaps I'd found him? It was with considerable trepidation that I walked up to his large house on the outskirts of town at the appointed time and rang the doorbell. I really had no idea what I would find on the other side of the door, but it was opened by a smiling and kindly looking elderly gentleman, tall and lean with a firm handshake. He invited me in to his study and immediately presented me with his book that he had written about his life, although when signing it to me he forgot that I was an Esau, not an Isaac. He quickly corrected his mistake and we talked about the early years of sawmilling in the Debolt area, he remembered my Dad and the dealings he had with Isaac and Esau Lumber Co.

During his time with Canfor in Grande Prairie he was tasked with finding a faster and more efficient method of milling smaller logs, and found what he called a 'Skragg Saw' in the U. S. It had two blades on one shaft set 4" apart with a flat chain running in a shallow trough along between the blades. A tall tooth set on the chain at 10 foot intervals hooked into the end of an 8 foot log and pulled it through the saws, creating a four inch wide Cant that was then laid on its side and put through an edger with blades set 2" apart to make ready to plane 2x4's. Roy bragged to me that with the introduction of this mill in Grande Prairie he was able to shut down six bush mills, an accomplishment that he was very proud of!

Although ours was not one of those six mills, Isaac and Esau Lumber Company's future was probably already predestined at that point. I saw no reason to turn our conversation into an uncomfortable one by reminding him his actions eventually led to the end of Isaac and Esau. By then, in my research, I had already learned a lot about why bush mills disappeared.

For many decades the bush mill was a viable way to produce lumber. The mill would set up in an area with lots of good timber and the logs would be skidded a short distance to the mill and then sawn into lumber, the product then hauled to market. Every few years as the timber in an area was used up the bush mill would be dismantled and moved to a new area. The houses, built on skids and never made too wide, were also skidded to the new location. With improved mechanization sawmills got larger and were using up logs at a much faster rate, necessitating the use of trucks to haul longer distances. Once the logs were loaded onto trucks it was more economical to haul them all the way into an urban area, to larger sawmills where there was a ready supply of labour, with workers responsible for their own housing. The mill no longer needed to be moved every few years, nor did its camp.

Another factor in the demise of the bush mill was the introduction of plywood plants which required the largest straightest logs, in direct competition with the bush mill. Particularly galling to the bush mill operator was often the fact that the plywood plant owner was also the owner of the rights to the timber being logged. They were required to pick out the best peeler logs, cut them into 8 ft. lengths and ship them off to the plywood plant, leaving the bush mill second rate saw logs. It was always a balancing act, ship enough of the peeler logs to keep the plant happy, yet retain enough good logs to make the bush mill viable. In the end Isaac and Esau Lumber Co. failed to make a living for all those involved and then Canfor seized all the equipment for what they claimed was money owing them. That was the End of Isaac and Esau Lumber Co. Ltd!

TWENTY ONE

BACK TO SIDE LAKE

Crossing the Simonette River on Quads

Robert and his son Scott on the first quad, Orlan and Judy Isaac on the right.

On August 30 2014 my siblings and I and some of our cousins made a quad trip back to Side Lake, we had tried five years earlier but the Simonette River was too high for the quads to cross. This time the water was much lower and we easily crossed over to the west side, climbed the bank and followed the old road south. After about ½ an hour of rough going we came to an old sawdust pile that was said to be the old Isaac and Esau sawmill site. I asked our guide where Side Lake was and he pointed south and said about ½ mile that way. My mind struggled to find any similarity between what I remembered about this place and what I was now confronted with, a very dense forest of mostly poplars, some of them quite large, where a clearing should have been. I had to remind myself that it had been 52 years since I had seen this place, trees can grow quite large in that much time. I was still quite skeptical.

There were well over 20 of us in this group of visitors, some of whom were locals and had been here recently, they pointed out old metal debris, tin cans, pails, unknown pieces of equipment that could have been sawmill parts etc. that were scattered throughout the nearby woods. My cousin Orlan had asked me earlier at the sawdust pile whether I thought we were at the actual Isaac and Esau site and I had replied that I was only about 50% sure. After finding all the metal stuff I grudgingly raised that to 60%! We were taken back up the road and over on the other side we were shown the scattered remains of some old school desks. On the way there I noticed an opening in the trees leading west, not a clearing so much as just an area with no large trees in it, just lots of low shrubs and small poplars. Standing on the old road it suddenly struck me, this could be the T intersection of the main road and Main Street! When one of the young men said they had found an old pipe sticking up out of the ground I really got excited and asked them to show me. It was located exactly where it should be, on the south side of the street just down from where the cook shack had been, this was the remains of our water well! That was when I knew for sure I was standing on Main Street! I paced west from the pipe and came to the place where our house had stood, we took a picture of me and my siblings on this spot. The school desk parts were also situated just to the north exactly where the old school had been, it was removed years earlier by a local farmer and used as a chicken coop! Most of the other buildings had been moved out to the next sawmill camp at Latornell River when Side Lake camp was abandoned.

We gathered up the metal remains of the old school desks and an old gas can etc. and took them with us as souvenirs.

The Esau siblings standing on the spot where our house was 50 years ago, from the left: Cameron, Jennifer, Marlene, Lenora and Robert.

TWENTY TWO

EPILOGUE

The Isaac brother's mother Anna Giesbrecht spent her last years living in the newly built Ridgevalley Home where she continued to be active making quilts. She claimed to have kept cancer in remission by eating crushed eggshells. She died July 22, 1978 at age 88.

My Mom, Pauline, suffered a slow demise because of MS, she spent her last years in the Linden Nursing Home where she passed away on May 25 1978.

My Grandfather John remained a partner in the Sawmill until 1952 although he and Grandma would occasionally live at camp for the winter, as they did in 1961 to 1962 when he drove the school van. He farmed his fields at Crooked Creek for many years, then seemingly always restless and wanting to find other opportunities they followed Alvies to Kelowna BC, still returning to the farm each spring and fall to plant and harvest his grain crop. Grandpa had a small woodworking shop and made stools etc., he also did a lot of carving, mostly chains out of a single piece of birch. After some years they moved to Medicine Hat, Alberta and then a few years later retired in Linden. He died of Cancer in Calgary June 14 1978, aged 82.

Philip farmed at his original homestead all his life, passing the farm on to his youngest son Orlan. Philip and Alda built a retirement home across the road from the old farmstead where they lived for many years. He suffered from balance issues and died March 12 1985, a day after falling off a trailer and receiving a serious head injury. He was age 70.

Peter was already having heart problems before he stopped lumbering, then after he sold out had to take it easy on himself. He died of a heart attack on Feb. 27, 1986 at his home in Crooked Creek at the age of 61.

Oliver lived in Edmonton working at various jobs, ending his working days by driving a pilot truck for wide loads and also delivering parts all over western Canada. He suffered from epilepsy and then later his kidneys failed him. He died April 26 1993, aged 71.

Henry moved his family to Abbotsford in 1965, where he drove truck, rolling one over and breaking his hip. He walked with a limp from then on. He and Margaret moved to Swanson Saskatchewan in 1980 where he once again homesteaded a quarter section of land, at age 64! He passed away on Sept 19 2003, at age 87

Edwin moved the family to Fort Vermilion for a few years, then down to Abbotsford in the lower Fraser valley. His next and last move was to Enderby, where he died on Aug. 28 2013 just before his 93rd birthday.

Alvie and his family moved to Kelowna, and then later to Medicine Hat. After retirement they lived in Grande Prairie, then in Red Deer, followed by living at his son's Rick house in Edmonton. He was residing in a hospital / old age home in Edmonton until he passed away in his sleep on November 22 2018, at age 93, the last of the "Company of Eight Men".

On the one year anniversary of Gordon's death I was living at Finley Forks and he was on my mind all day, the same had happened earlier for Donald. It surprised me that a whole year had gone by and I was still functioning every day, getting on with life. It took many years before an anniversary would go by and I would only remember later that it had come and gone.

I seldom talked about them and sometimes when I did I would get emotional but not always, depended on my mood and who I was talking to. I got on with my life and when I left the family a second time I moved to Vancouver and put in a full career as a transit bus driver, then followed that up with driving school bus. I got married (twice!) and have two sons and a daughter of whom I'm very proud, and two granddaughters all of whom live nearby and who I get to see often. I kept moving east from Vancouver into the suburbs, always seeking a quieter life in the country as opposed to the rat race of living and working in the city. I am now retired and live in the country in Maple Ridge listening to music from the 60's, writing, woodworking, and volunteering with a service club.

Cameron in 1964

APPENDIX ONE

BOARD FOOT MEASURE (BFM)

Board Foot Measure, (BFM) is a specialized unit of measure for the volume of lumber, it is the volume of a one-foot length of board one foot wide and one inch thick, or 144 cubic inches of wood. A 2 x 4 at a foot & 1/2 long, or a 2 X 12 at only 6" long would both be one BFM, so a 12 foot long 2 X 4 would be 8 BFM and a 12 foot long 2 X 12 would be 24 BFM. The mill produced lumber in a large variety of sizes and lengths, 1 inch boards 4 and 6 inches wide, and 2" planks at 4, 6, 8, 10, and 12 inch widths. A 2 X 10 at 7 and ¼ inches long is just over one BFM, so how many BFM in a 2 X 10 16 feet long? (26.666) With this in mind you can see the challenge in adding up the volume of lumber as it goes by you on a green chain as I describe in chapter Fifteen!

APPENDIX TWO

HISTORY OF CATERPILLAR

The steam tractors of the 1890s and early 1900s were extremely heavy, sometimes weighing 1,000 pounds (450kg) per horsepower, and often sank into the rich, soft earth of the farmland. A solution considered was to lay a temporary plank road ahead of the steam tractor, but this was time-consuming, expensive, and interfered with earthmoving. Benjamin Holt of California thought of wrapping the planks around the wheels. He replaced the wheels on a 40 horsepower Holt steamer with a set of wooden tracks bolted to chains. In 1904 he successfully tested the updated machine plowing some soggy delta land. A photographer reported to have observed that the tractor crawled like a caterpillar and Holt seized on the metaphor, "Caterpillar it is. That's the name for it!"

The C.L. Best Tractor Company, an early pioneer of gas engines and tracked machines, made the "Best 60" which became the most successful tractor in their line. After the 1925 merger of the Best's Company and the Holt Manufacturing Company that formed the Caterpillar Tractor Company, the Best 60 was renamed the Caterpillar Sixty. The name Caterpillar was registered by Holt in 1910.

In the meantime Cleveland Motor Plow Co. at Cleveland, Ohio, while waiting for a patent on a motor plough, shifted their focus to crawler-type tractors. The inspiration for the "Cleveland" crawler of 1916 came from an experimental version of the C.L. Best Gas Traction Company's 8-16 horse-power "Pony" tracklayer (equipped with continuous roller belts over cogged wheels). The following year the company changed its name to the Cleveland Tractor Co. and in 1918 the little crawler became known as the "Cletrac". In the 1920s, crawler tractors were gaining in popularity, especially Cletracs, they were advertised as 'Geared to the ground'. They were excellent tractors, sold well, and remained a popular make until the end of the company in the 1940s. Cletracs were mostly powered by gas engines, then in 1933, following Caterpillar's example, diesel engines were introduced as an option.

A bulldozer is a continuous tracked tractor equipped with a substantial metal plate (known as a dozer) used to push large quantities of soil, sand, rubble, or other such material during construction or logging. The term "bulldozer" is often used erroneously to mean any heavy equipment (sometimes a loader and sometimes an excavator), but precisely, the term refers only to a tractor (usually tracked) fitted with a dozer blade. Winches were affixed to the rear of tractors to facilitate the skidding of logs in logging operations. In 1945, Caterpillar introduced its first bulldozer straight blades operated by cable control units. Its angle blades were introduced in the following year. They next offered hydraulic controlled blades in 1947.

Caterpillar first introduced the RD4 in 1936 as the diesel follow up to the successful CAT 30 gas model. The RD4 originally weighed in at 10,000 pounds, and used Caterpillar's D4400 engine, producing about 43HP at the drawbar. In 1935 Caterpillar had started the naming convention of "RD" for diesel or "R" for regular gasoline, followed by a number to indicate the relative engine size, so the 4 indicated the relative engine power. In 1937 the "R" was dropped, and just a "D" was used for the diesel versions. The later D4 series engines quickly increased in power, so the number "4" just became a figure of merit rather than indicating actual engine power. During World War II Caterpillar products found fame with the construction battalions of the United States army and navy, they were used extensively in the building of the Alaska Highway.

APPENDIX THREE

THE LOGGING TRUCK

The International Harvester Company built its first truck in 1909. Over the years, International's triple-diamond logo became widely associated with tough, hard-working vehicles. In 1952, International could still claim that over half the vehicles it ever built were still in service.

The K and KB trucks were introduced in the mid 1940's. They were best known for their durability, prewar design in a postwar era, and low price. The follow-up to the K, the KB, was introduced in 1947, with the characteristic difference being a widened lower grill appearing like "wings", and moving of the triple-diamond badge from the front of the nose to the top of the grille plus adding the model designation to the hood sides. They used a center hinged butterfly hood rather than the rear hinged hood of the smaller trucks.

The KB-7 had a basic rating of 2-3 tons, a GVW rating of 16,500 lb., and a GCW rating of 29,000 lb. The engine was the 100-hp Blue Diamond BLD-269, putting its power through a standard 5-speed transmission and a single-speed rear axle.

International Harvester was best known for its farm equipment, binders and combines etc. As a result the trucks earned the sobriquet 'cornbinder'. For the purpose of using them as logging trucks, they were transformed into arch trucks, the first one having been made by Dads cousin Eddie Dierker and used at one of our north camps. The deck on the truck was removed and replaced with an inclining frame of two large beams (approx. 1 ft. square) mounted from just behind the cab on either side and resting up on blocks at the back end of the frame so that the protruding ends were about 8 ft. off the ground. A large wheel block (pulley) was attached to a cross beam so that a cable from a winch mounted just behind the cab could be strung up and over the pulley. This cable was then slung around the butt ends of a bundle of logs and when the winch was retracted it raised the ends of the logs off of the ground and the whole bundle could then be dragged to the mill. When the driver attempted to haul too large a load the front end of the truck would rise into the air as the winch was retracted, then bounce back down as the winch was slacked off. Sometimes with a large load the same thing would happen when the clutch was released and the truck started to move forward, then the driver would depress the clutch to allow the front end of the truck to drop back to the ground, and again release the clutch to start to move forward and slowly the truck would gain momentum going straight ahead until the front end would finally settle solidly on to the ground to facilitate steering!

GLOSSARY

Bucking – cutting up of a felled and de-limbed tree into shorter logs.

BFM - stands for Board Foot Measure, more commonly known as Board Foot, see appendix one.

Canters – Mill workers who rolled the logs on to the carriage and fastened them with the dogs.

Cant Hook – tool with the same premise as the peavey but with blunt teeth-bearing tip. A Cant Hook is a traditional logging tool consisting of a wooden lever handle with a movable metal hook called a dog at one end, used for handling, rolling and moving logs. Unlike the similar peavey, the cant hook has a blunt tip, often bearing teeth on the same side as the swiveled hook.

Cat skinner – operator of a cat, or crawler tractor (see sidebar on Caterpillar)

Chinook - Chinook winds often called chinooks commonly refers to winds in the interior West of North America, where the Canadian Prairies and Great Plains meet various mountain ranges. Chinook is claimed by popular folk-etymology to mean "eater", but it is really the name of the people in the region where the usage was first derived. The reference to a wind or weather system, simply "a Chinook", originally meant a warming wind from the ocean into the interior regions. A strong Chinook can make snow one foot deep almost vanish in one day. The snow partly melts and partly evaporates in the dry wind. Chinook winds have been observed to raise winter temperature, often from below -20°C (-4°F) to as high as 10-20°C (50-68°F) for a few hours or days, then temperatures plummet to their base levels. Chinooks are most prevalent over southern Alberta, but they can and do occur annually as far north as High Level.

Choker man – a bush worker who works in close proximity to a cat, dragging chokers to the butt ends of logs and fastening them around the log then hooking the other end to the winch cable of the cat.

Cletrack – an early type of crawler tractor manufactured by Cleveland Tractor Co. (see Appendix two)

Conscientious Objectors – (CO) is an "individual who has claimed the right to refuse to perform military service" on the grounds of freedom of thought, conscience, and/or religion. In Canada, CO's are assigned to an alternative civilian service as a substitute for conscription or military service. Some CO's consider themselves pacifist, non-interventionist, non-resistant, or antimilitarist.

Cracklings - When butchering a pig the fat cut off of the meat was ground up and boiled in a large pot (rendered) and the small pieces of meat left over in the fat floated to the top. This was cracklings, served on toast with beet syrup or on pancakes, or mixed in with fried potatoes for breakfast.

Edger - A piece of mill equipment with blades set at various distances apart used to trim the rough edges of a board or plank to make a finished edge. Several of the blades were adjustable to various widths, controlled by the Edger-man as needed.

Edger-man - Mill worker responsible for lining up and pushing the rough sawn planks through the edger.

Faller - Worker out in the forest responsible for felling trees.

Felling – process of cutting down a standing tree.

Frezno - A hand handled scoop pulled by horses or mules used for moving dirt when roadbuilding etc.

Green chain - Two flat chains moving along parallel to each other about 8 or 10 feet apart, along which the finished lumber would move along slowly, to be sorted and piled on to individual stacks by the lumber piler.

Hand Felling saws - were used to fell the trees, it is generally less stiff and has a narrower blade than a hand bucking saw allowing wedges to be more easily inserted, preventing the kerf from closing on the saw.

Sawyer – Mill worker responsible for controlling the carriage and log as it moved through the main saw, he was the most skilled worker in the mill and set the pace of work being done.

Scaling – measurement of logs to determine the volume of merchantable wood

Skidding – transportation of logs from the site of felling to the landing along the ground

Stooking – The piling up of sheaves of grain in a pyramid shape to help in drying out the grain and keeping it from moulding on the ground.

Tail-edger man – Mill worker responsible for receiving the planks after they have gone through the edger.

Tail sawyer – Mill worker responsible for receiving the plank off the carriage after it had been sawn and separating the slabs from the good planks and passing the planks on to the Edgerman.

Trimmer man – Mill worker responsible for trimming the ends off planks to make a finished piece of lumber.

SOURCE NOTES

Across The Smokey, published by Debolt and District Pioneer Museum Society, 1978

Bridges to the Past, published by Debolt and District Pioneer Museum Society, 2001

Working in the Woods by Ken Drushka, 1992

Memoirs and Poems by Henry Isaac

Writings of John Esau

Writings of Edwin Esau

Writings of Florence Isaac

Postscript by Clarence Esau

Wikipedia

CPSIA information can be obtained
at www.ICGtesting.com
Printed in the USA
BVHW090037201220
596041BV00006B/26

9 781525 577369